A young woman's journey across one of the world's most patriarchal lands

ARABELA IGGESEN VALENZUELA

For privacy reasons, some names, locations, and dates may have been changed.

ISBN: 979-8-9886732-1-7 (Paperback)
ISBN: 979-8-9886732-0-0 (eBook)

Library of Congress Control Number: 2023913189

First edition 2023

Published by The Spicy Travel Girl
Anaheim, CA, USA

For more information, visit the author's website at
www.thespicytravelgirl.com

This book is dedicated to the people of Balochistan, who despite unimaginable hardships persevere every day and continue to extend the greatest hospitality to their guests.

The beauty of Balochistan

CONTENTS

PREFACE

Being born into a multicultural family, I have never known a life without travel. Since infanthood, I have flown across oceans and continents to visit loved ones and spend holidays together. As a teenager, I moved from Germany to the United States, and later to China for studies. I found great independence when I started solo traveling at age sixteen. I spent every free minute planning and saving money for the breaks in between semesters as I developed an insatiable hunger to see more of the world. While the great privilege of travel is widely associated with luxury and voyeurism, I began to view it as part of my education. Learning about the world's people, places, and cultures was not a waste of time but the greatest investment I could make to my personal development.

My way of traveling changed when I moved to Pakistan in 2020. The country was unlike any place I had been before. From its vast diversity of landscapes, cultures, and languages to the traditional values and lifestyles that many Pakistani people still adhere to, the country's unique attributes inspired me to slow down and spend more time getting to know the people and cultures. I abandoned any notions of comfort as I faced temperatures ranging from -20°C to +50°C, slept in buses, barns, and construction sites, and shared roofs with dozens of people and animals.

Around this time, I launched a travel blog focused on solo female adventure travel, with the aim of sharing my experiences of some of the more offbeat corners of the globe. By the beginning of 2022, I had visited dozens of fascinating places in all provinces and territories of Pakistan and met people from countless castes, sects, and social ranks. I am beyond grateful for these experiences.

After these two years I thought I had experienced it all and become immune to culture shocks. Then, Balochistan happened. Straddling the nations of Pakistan, Iran, and Afghanistan, Balochistan is a vast, arid, and sparsely populated land on the border between the Middle East and South Asia. Home to a variety of peoples, Balochistan is primarily inhabited by the Baloch ethnic group, an Iranic people with a unique culture, distinct from the neighboring Persians or peoples of the Indian subcontinent. Balochi culture and practices vary significantly between geographic regions, tribes, sub-tribes, and religious sects, but most Baloch people share the commonalities of extraordinary artisanal skills, strict codes of honor and hospitality, and a largely conservative, patriarchal culture.

Unfortunately, life for the people of Balochistan is anything but easy. The region accounts for the most impoverished and underdeveloped provinces of both Pakistan and Iran, widely lacking access to healthcare, education, and vital resources, despite its rich natural reserves. The region is frequently the victim of natural disaster—floods, droughts, and heatwaves—,and is plagued by political instability caused by clashes between the various players in the region. To protect its interests, the Pakistani government in recent years has all but banned foreign travelers from Balochistan, requiring them to obtain special permission to visit. This makes the region off-limits for many tourists, and foreigners are a very rare sight.

I had been to Balochistan before, on brief day trips to some of the region's natural attractions situated along its beautiful coastline. During those visits, accompanied by male travelers, I got a glimpse of Baloch hospitality, but experienced very little of the local culture and lifestyle. Things were completely different when I visited Balochistan in the summer of 2022 on an overland journey from Pakistan to Iran. Not only did I have the chance to travel more extensively across the land but visiting all alone as a woman in this deeply patriarchal part of the world proved to be a vastly different experience from all my previous trips. When I returned, I knew I had to share my experiences with the world. I began working on a blog post but soon realized that I had far too much to share to fit into an online article—and so the idea for this book was born.

Of Threads and Needles is my first travel memoir. I wrote it to share my stories of this lesser-visited region from the unique perspective of a solo female traveler. The book explores my personal struggle of culture shock and self-identity, but also exposes various injustices I witnessed during this trip. By no means do I intend to criticize Baloch culture and customs, and I have attempted to convey my personal thoughts and experiences with as much cultural sensitivity as possible. All names mentioned are pseudonyms and I have made minor adjustments to some details in order to protect the privacy of the people I encountered. Furthermore, I tried to give explanations for all non-English terms I use throughout this book; however, if there is any confusion, feel free to refer to the glossary at the end of the book.

Arabela (Bela) Urpi Iggesen Valenzuela

A wedding in Lasbela

Tehran
Qom
Iran
Kerman
Afghanistan
Balochistan
Pakistan
Persian Gulf
Dubai
Gulf of Oman
Darak
Gabd-Rimdan Border
Chabahar
Surbandar
Gwadar
Pasni
Kund Malir
Lasbela
Karachi
Arabian Sea

CHAPTER ONE

A HUNDRED WEAPONS

"Having a woman with you in Balochistan is like traveling with a hundred weapons. Nobody will dare to harm you if you are with a woman. That's how much Baloch men respect women."

This phrase, spoken by a strange man during one of my previous trips to Balochistan, was all that could quench my nerves on this scorching summer afternoon in June 2022. The humidity struck me as I climbed out of my air-conditioned taxi at Aath Chowk, Lyari, and suddenly found myself immersed in a noisy market-like atmosphere in Karachi's most notorious neighborhood. The yells of touts and vendors were nearly as loud as the honks from the cars and buses around us. The stench of garbage and animal waste was even more pungent than I remembered from my previous visit. I looked up to the claustrophobia-inducing multi-story residential buildings and wondered what kinds of people might live in the oldest and most densely populated part of the city. Lyari used to be Karachi's infamous hotspot of crime and gang violence, but locals assured me that the situation had since improved and the neighborhood was gradually transitioning into a center for artists and creatives.

My driver carefully got out of his seat and helped me carry my suitcase into the waiting room of the nearest van stand, an informal terminal for small buses and vans. I looked over my shoulder a few times to check for pickpockets. Then, I pulled out my wallet, counted my cash for the fare in fifty-rupee notes, and handed the money to the driver. We exchanged formal goodbyes and he drove away, leaving me standing in the middle of a chaotic bus terminal. It was at that moment that I realized, from now on, I would be alone.

I should have been more excited. This was the starting point of a trip I had been fantasizing about my entire life. Since my childhood, I had dreamed of Iran. I was enchanted by the ancient ruins of Persepolis and the sparkling Abbasid-era architecture and dreamed of strolling across traditional bazaars and listening to the language of great Sufi poets. Footage of the exquisite natural and cultural richness of this Middle Eastern treasure chest evoked strong feelings of wanderlust in me, and all I wanted to do was follow the footsteps of caravan traders of ancient times and embark on a reverse journey of the Hippie Trail. Finally, after several long years of dreaming, planning, and waiting, the time was just right. I was on summer break from university, had meager but sufficient savings, and happened to already be spending my days in neighboring Pakistan. And not long before, a new border crossing between Pakistan and Iran had been inaugurated, opening a direct route from Karachi by road. The coincidence seemed nothing short of a divine sign to me. I had to take this chance. With more than two thousand kilometers worth of stunning nature, culture, and architecture awaiting me, I had more than enough reasons to be euphoric. However, at the same time, I also felt quite nervous.

The nervousness stemmed almost entirely from one concern: Balochistan. Nestled between the sparsely populated border regions of Pakistan, Iran, and Afghanistan lies this vast yet often forgotten stretch of land. The region is home to the Baloch people, an ethnic group with an identity distinct from any other people in the region. While the land is rich in culture and resources, little of this wealth is apparent at first glance. Balochistan is the most impoverished and underdeveloped region in both Pakistan and Iran; natural disasters strike often and badly, and political unrest is so widespread that the Pakistani government prohibits foreigners from traveling to the region without special permission.

But these were not my main concerns. I had been on brief trips to Balochistan before and was convinced I could deal with all of that. A trusted friend had promised to arrange my permission, as he had done for previous trips, and guaranteed that I would be safe from targeted attacks and kidnappings. What I was truly worried about was the culture, where a very conservative, deeply patriarchal mindset dominates. On my earlier visits I noticed the streets were empty of women. Baloch families, while extremely welcoming and hospitable, enforced strict gender roles that typically restricted women to their homes. Options for women were limited, and while I had the privilege of ignoring these realities while in the company of outsider men, I dwelled on how I would fare this time, traveling alone. I had the help of some local contacts who had offered to host me in their homes, but with no proper guardian by my side— no father, brother, or husband to accompany me throughout the journey, which is an unwritten requirement in this part of the world. And while traveling alone was certainly no novelty to me, visiting one of the world's most patriarchal places as a solo female traveler was.

To say that people (read: men) had tried to dissuade me from this undertaking would be an understatement. Their responses ranged from rather animatedly explaining why it was unsafe, to claiming it was entirely impossible. I recalled the concerns of my Baloch friends when I first shared my plan with them: "Don't go to Balochistan by yourself. You will not be safe as a woman traveling alone." But despite everything, I dismissed their concerns. I wanted to think it was because of my principles—the principles I had developed when I first started traveling alone at age sixteen—that women could do anything by themselves, and fear could not control my decisions. How could I be an inspirational figure for women if I scratched my carefully crafted plans to travel overland to Iran because of the opinions of some men? Certainly, they all just subconsciously desired to control women, I thought. Letting their fearmongering get in the way of an empowered woman's plans would only feed into the oppressive structures of patriarchy, I told myself. Besides, if Baloch men truly respected women like a hundred weapons, what was the worst that could happen, anyway?

The choice was clear. Instead of risking a personal defeat to my ego, and perhaps fueled by a hint of naiveté, I decided to carry on with my plans. Nothing could halt me from chasing my dream, including the nervosity in my veins.

I dragged my heavy dress towards the cool main waiting hall of the van stand, where my luggage sat, only to be directed by the ticket seller to a small, dusty room without air-conditioning. Inside the room waited another woman and her little son, who both seemed to be waiting there for the same van. Without saying a word, I sat down on the floor next to them.

I felt extremely hot. Not so much because of the temperature or the lack of air-conditioning but because of my clothes. I was wearing a traditional Balochi women's outfit: a three-piece suit consisting of baggy trousers (shalwar); a long, thick dress (pashk) with an embroidered front pouch (pendol); and a huge scarf designed to cover a woman's body from head to toe (chadar). Every piece of clothing was skillfully embroidered with traditional dooch designs, intricate geometric shapes crafted onto fabric with nothing but a thread and a needle. Like most Baloch women, I also covered my face in public. While many women would opt for an Islamic face shield (niqab), I wore a cloth or surgical mask, or would drape my chadar around my mouth and nose to achieve the same effect.

On paper, none of this was necessary. Officially, there was no dress code for any place in Pakistan, except for religious sites, and I theoretically could have minimized the amount of fabric on my body to a t-shirt and yoga pants, as any European would do as soon as the temperature hit 20°C, yet I knew this would have been unwise. After all, I was alone and I could not allow myself any more attention than necessary in this vulnerable situation. Hence, I tried hard to blend in with the crowd—easier said than done for someone who had grown up in a completely different culture.

As sweat dripped down my makeshift niqab, I glanced at the other woman, who was also wearing a plain black outer garment called an abaya on top of her traditional dress. I could not imagine how hot she must have felt in this sticky room, yet her facial expression seemed completely calm as she gently caressed her baby boy. She must have been as immune to this unbearable heat as Americans are to freezing-cold air-conditioning.

Outside of the sticky room, I listened to the yells of ticket vendors and van drivers, who recruited most of their passengers on the spot. I felt irked as I heard one of them yell, "Bela, Bela, Bela." I held my breath, then realized that the man was merely touting the final destination of their route—Lasbela—to other customers; not catcalling me. I let out a relieved sigh and leaned back against the dirty walls. Vans in Pakistan have no fixed departure times but instead leave whenever they are full. There was little I could do but wait silently in the heat and hope that a few more souls had plans to go to Lasbela that afternoon.

After a few minutes, which felt like hours, the ticket seller gestured for me and the other lady to come out of the stuffy waiting room as our van was full and ready to leave. I checked to ensure my face was covered properly by my cheap fabric mask and adjusted my intricately embroidered white chadar to wrap tightly around my face yet flow loosely around my silhouette. Once every yard of fabric appeared to be in its right place, I followed the woman and her child into the noisy street and we made our way towards the van.

When the van driver saw us, he waved us to the back row, the bumpiest row of the vehicle, which is usually reserved for women and families, while the rows in front of us were quickly filled up by dozens of men. I looked around and felt relief: It was only the three of us in the back row. This meant I had more than three feet of personal space, a rare luxury in Pakistani public transportation. The van departed and I enjoyed the bumpy yet unusually comfortable journey in the back row as the driver stopped every few minutes to pick up more passengers.

Block by block, we slowly passed through the dense urban jungle of Lyari, where boys were playing soccer in the narrow enclosures between their colorful residential compounds and fully veiled women were carrying sacks of vegetables and grains between the cows and chickens on the road. Cloth vendors and rickshaw drivers were loudly pitching their offers to any soul that moved. The van accelerated as we left Lyari behind and entered the barren industrial outskirts of Karachi, where clouds of toxic fumes entered through the van's windows from every direction. Whether they were coming from textile mills or food-processing plants or any of the hundreds of grey industrial compounds, each cloud had a distinctly pungent fragrance that pierced through the tiny interstices of my cloth mask. Far behind the endless layers of polluted sky, I eventually recognized the premises of the Yousuf Goth transportation hub, where our van slowed to a near full stop in the miles of traffic jam caused by the countless coasters heading to Balochistan. In the middle of the chaos, I spotted a woman holding an infant in her arm. She was selling embroidered chadars to the passengers on the buses. Seeing the sweat dripping from her face, I wished I could have bought one of her beautiful scarves, yet as soon as she got close to my window, the driver took off as it was now our turn to cross the toll plaza. Without a glance, the uniformed men at the adjacent Sindh Police booth waived us through. After all, we were coming from Karachi and going to Balochistan, not vice-versa. We swiftly crossed the Hub River, which officially marks the end of Karachi and the beginning of Balochistan.

Throughout this relatively relaxed first portion of the journey, I had nearly taken for granted the luck of my empty back row in a crowded van. However, my bliss abruptly ended when a family of seven joined the row in Hub Chowki, the first town of Balochistan. Suddenly, I found myself squeezed into the corner by a group of laughing women with children on their laps whose cries overshadowed even the loud sounds of the engines. The youngest member of the group was a newborn baby while the oldest one was a frail-looking but constantly smiling elderly woman. She was the only woman on the bus whose face was not covered by fabric, revealing her prominent one-inch-diameter nose pin and the unique tribal-style tattoo on her chin. Body modifications seemed to play a role in the family's women's lives, as even their toddler daughter had cotton threads woven through her earlobes. They looked like they had been pierced just a few days prior.

Like commonly seen on local vans, the women were gossiping loudly in Balochi while passing around a bag of dried fruits and nuts, seemingly completely unbothered by the intense heat generated by all the bodies. They offered their snacks to me, but I declined, afraid of being struck up in a conversation in a language I did not understand. Despite their pleasantly bubbly presence, I leaned outside the open window to breathe in some fresh air and distance myself at least a little from the newly arrived crowd. As their thighs, waists, elbows, and shoulders were pressing tightly against mine, for once I felt grateful for the long garments the women were all wearing, these being the only barrier from each other's sweat in this hot and crowded van.

In the following hour, we passed miles and miles of green mangroves and the golden Kirthar Mountains, which, riddled with holes and caves, are a unique characteristic of the Hub area. We were moving at a significantly faster speed at this point, mainly because in the sparsely populated land of Balochistan there were few passengers to pick up. We continued on the well-paved road until the landscape began to flatten into a desert-like environment and camels appeared from all corners. As the terrain began to change in colors and textures, so did my mood. I suddenly felt my nervousness dissipate into the vast emptiness and be replaced by anticipation. Instead of silently suffering in the crowd and heat, I now excitedly imagined all the adventures I was about to experience over the next couple of weeks while in this gorgeous land.

Little did I anticipate just how different this solo trip would be from my previous visits to Balochistan. Not being accompanied by a man, I would live experiences far from anything I had ever witnessed before. Being exposed to a more realistic perspective of the lives of the silent half of the population, I would panic as my privilege slipped away from beneath my feet and cry about realities far beyond my scope of comprehension. Instead of another voyeuristic leisure trip, this journey would become one of my most eye-opening experiences

I'd ever have. Nothing in the world could prepare me for the culture shock I was about to experience. After all, few women had done what I was doing by venturing alone through one of the world's most patriarchal cultures. Locals had warned me, outsiders had shaken their heads, and fellow travelers were simply baffled. Yet, here I was—a stubborn twenty-one-year-old girl with a will of steel who was ready to jump headfirst into the freezing waters of uncertainty to pursue her dreams.

CHAPTER TWO

NO BAD INFLUENCES

Not long after, our van pulled into a side street at the entrance of a smallish town. We had finally arrived in Lasbela, the first stop of my journey. I quickly made my way out of the crowded back row and gathered my belongings. A man climbed on the roof of the vehicle to unfasten my suitcase and pass it down to me. Once I had retrieved all my belongings, the driver honked a few times, and before I could look around, the van had already left, continuing its journey deep into the heart of Balochistan.

As soon as I stepped out onto the dusty road, I was surrounded by hundreds of eyes. They belonged to men offering everything from bottled water to rickshaw rides, or simply waiting for the next vehicle. Every single one of them was clothed in the characteristic Balochi men's suit with *shalwar* so baggy they nearly touched the ground and colorfully embroidered caps. Some had wet cloths draped around their heads to help them cool down in the scorching heat. Using a water bottle, I also wet my face mask to achieve a similar effect.

Being the only woman in a sea of men felt frightening, but I tried not to let the fear get to me by reminding myself what I'd been told earlier about Baloch men respecting women and not daring to harm them. And so far, I had been accorded only full respect. In the crowd of men, I heard no catcalls or wolf whistles. Nobody tried to touch me or talk to me, and the men did not stare in an intense, perverted way, but merely in a neutral, non-malicious manner. Most likely, they were just looking for potential customers and had no bad intentions. My reflex, however, was to hide. A bit of extra modesty has never harmed me. I pulled my *chadar* further down my face and reversed the game: I could watch people without being seen. Sometimes, a piece of fabric really does wonders.

I observed the crowd of men for a good while until a series of loud honks redirected my attention. I turned my head and caught sight of a massive vehicle. My host, Jalal, and his nephew, Sanaullah, had arrived! They had come in their silver Land Rover this time, just one of the many pickup trucks they owned. Using hand gestures, Jalal signaled for me to get into the back of the vehicle, while Sanaullah got out to help with my luggage.

I had known Jalal for about half a year. I first met this mysterious middle-aged man on an earlier trip to Balochistan, during which he hosted me and a companion in his luxurious guesthouse in Lasbela. When he learned about my plans to travel to Iran overland, he offered to host me once more and accompany me across the border. Of course, his support was well appreciated. Not only did I know I would have to rely on the families of acquaintances to host me in their homes, since many hotels would refuse to rent a room to an unaccompanied woman, but I was also excited to admire the beauty of the coastal road from the comfort of a spacious private car. Hence, I accepted his invitation and made his hometown the first stop of my journey.

From the outside, Jalal appeared tough, if not downright intimidating. He was a very big and muscle-packed man who looked like he could devour an entire goat in a single meal. His face was rugged and tanned from the scorching desert, and the lines around his forehead looked like they had been drawn with kohl. He always seemed to be surrounded by weapons, from heavy Kalashnikovs over each shoulder to hand pistols in each of his pockets; there existed not a single photo of him without a gun.

Contrary to his outward appearance, Jalal had the warmest heart of any man I had ever met in Pakistan. From the moment we first met, he had impressed me with his respectful behavior.

He was the only man I had ever known who could make his guests feel like royalty, family, and childhood best friends all at the same time. I recalled dinners spent rolling on the floor laughing at his jokes, yet when the situation demanded, he could be as distant as a stranger, granting me all the space I needed as the only woman in the group.

Jalal loved his sons, especially his eldest, Umair, who was eleven. He was a proud father and never shy to hide his love for his family from the world. However, he never mentioned a word about any of the women in his family, as it would have been a sign of disrespect had he discussed them in front of strangers.

Being a *sardar*, or local landlord, Jalal was blessed with many luxuries that most local families could only dream of. The huge cars, houses, guns, and vast areas of land that outsiders get to see are but an appetizer of the wealth of the *sardars* of poverty-stricken Balochistan. Ownership of the land, which typically comes with significant local influence and involvement in politics, is passed down from generation to generation, establishing a distinct social hierarchy in the region. Today, it is Jalal who travels across the region, looks after the people, and is involved in official affairs; tomorrow it will be his son's responsibility, and their families will likely enjoy lifelong privileges compared to most ordinary people in the area. *Sardars* are the nobility in the feudalist system that exists in Balochistan to this day.

Barely my senior, Sanaullah was the complete opposite of his uncle. From the outside, he perfectly fit the description of the nice boy next door: tall in stature yet as slender as a prepubescent boy, with a slim, bony face shaped by a prominent jawline and high cheekbones, with innocent-looking brown eyes that seemed to have never seen a vice. His demeanor was courteous and shy, a rare trait amongst sons of influential families. Throughout my previous visit, he never said a single word and just quietly followed us around. He was always there to help but had no demands of his own. However, behind his soft, shy, and innocent appearance, a tough character was hiding. He was an extremely skilled fighter, proficient in all kinds of weaponry. He could change bullets within seconds and aim at targets moving faster than race cars. I first noticed this when we went shooting in the mountains during our last trip and he did not miss a single shot; instead, he blasted each and every rock he aimed at into a thousand pieces. Like his uncle, he enjoyed hunting. They went to the mountains every weekend to hunt rabbits and ibexes. Sanaullah then skinned the animals and chopped them up into pieces like a butcher. After gathering dry twigs and wood, he ignited a fire using just his hands as tools. Whatever meat is considered *halal*, or permissible by Islamic standards, he cooked over the open flame to fuel the exhausted muscles of the hungry men, while the meat that is considered *haram*, or impermissible, he fed to his animals. Whoever travels with Sanaullah is guaranteed to survive in the wilderness, as this young man was not only skilled and strong but also fearless and ready to defend his people from all dangers, whether wild animals or humans. No wonder Jalal took him instead of a bodyguard on most of his adventures.

In one skillful throw, Sanaullah landed my hefty suitcase in the loading area of the car. Following this raw display of strength, he cautiously opened the back door of the vehicle for me like an old-school gentleman. Behind his militaristically stiff expression I noticed a shy smile as he greeted me with a barely audible "*asalam-o-aleikum.*" I climbed into my seat and let him close the door. Immediately, I felt the relief of cool air on my sweaty face. Jalal's spacious, air-conditioned Land Rover was the exact opposite of the cramped, sweltering van where I had spent the last couple of hours. I lay back and made myself comfortable as we began the drive to Jalal's guesthouse.

The dense swarms of rickshaws, donkey carts, and pedestrians clouding the roads instantly dissipated as we made our way through Lasbela. Jalal is known and respected by everyone in town and so are his guests. When one of his vehicles appears on the road, every other commuter yields way, like to an ambulance with blaring sirens. I was sitting in the back seat, where the windows had dark shades, able to observe the outside while the outside could not see me. Peeking through the shades, I watched as we drove by schools and pharmacies, tuck shops and street stalls, goats, and donkeys. There were lots of men of all ages around, mostly selling their goods or working in one of the many roadside businesses. Eventually, the commercial area thinned out, and we approached rows and rows of sand-colored one-story buildings. Instead of yelling vendors and honking rickshaws, we were now surrounded by laughing children and barking dogs playing with simple toys in the soft desert sand, and even a couple of women doing chores in front of their houses.

At the end of the road, I spotted a familiar building. It was Jalal's guest house, where I had stayed during my last visit. While I was expecting we had arrived at our destination, Jalal suddenly made a sharp turn towards a residential block and drove a few houses in.

"Since you came by yourself this time, I've decided to take you to my family's home instead," he announced with a bright smile. "My wife will host you and you will get to meet my daughters."

We pulled up to a large gate and I got out of the truck. Sanaullah swiftly unloaded the bags and dropped them off in front of the gate, where Jalal picked them up and carried them inside the property. I followed him through the gate, passing by a forest of colorful embroidered women's dresses neatly hanging in the sun to dry. At last, we reached his inconspicuous-looking family residence, which looked nothing like I had imagined the family home of an influential feudal lord to be. Unlike the shiny palaces and gardens where the nobility of the world resides, the family's home looked no different from the neighboring sand-colored clay and brick houses, just bigger and with a garage for SUVs instead of a barn for animals.

In front of the house, a group of women and girls stood lined up, some of whom appeared to be around the same age as Jalal, while others seemed a few years younger than me. They greeted me with handshakes, hugs, and kisses, and showered me in pleasantries so quickly that my mind could not keep up. Jalal introduced them to me as his wife, sister, daughters, and nieces. While I was still receiving greetings from some, I could see the wife rushing into a small cubicle near the entrance of the house, and Jalal quietly disappeared to the opposite side of the property. Three of the girls excitedly grabbed my hand and ushered me to their room, while the others followed suit, with my belongings in tow. In a matter of seconds, the family's warm reception dissipated any remaining doubts I had about going to Balochistan.

The room we entered looked a little different from a typical girl's room in Karachi. Not too large and not too small, tidy and clutter-free, with only the most essential objects in sight, which made the room appear quite spacious. There was one king-sized bed on one side, which was neatly covered with a *rilli*, a type of patchwork blanket commonly found across southern Pakistan.

On the other side of the room, there was a large carpet and a couple of cylinder-shaped pillows called *takya.* On the adjacent wall, there were wardrobes and cabinets filled to the brim with *pashk* and cosmetic products. Across from that, the girls carefully dropped off my belongings in a straight line like tin soldiers. There was no air-conditioning, and the fan was not on, likely due to load-shedding, but the windowless room shielded us well enough from the heat outside.

Once all the daughters and nieces had entered the room, they asked me to sit down on the bed next to them and make myself comfortable. "Take off your *chadar,*" one of the daughters urged me. "Don't you have a *dupatta* to wear inside the house?"

Before I could answer her question, another girl rushed to the cabinet and pulled out a light, orange-colored scarf with black cross-stitch embroidery. "We are all girls here, you can feel comfortable and make yourself at home," they brightly proclaimed.

One after another, Jalal's daughters and nieces introduced themselves by name, age, and relation to my host. All seven of them seemed to be well-educated and aged somewhere between 13 and 17 years. They were all dressed in traditional Balochi suits, covered from head to toe with intricate *dooch,* with their collars stuck together by shiny gold-plated brooches. Every color of the rainbow could be found in their dresses, which came in various types of light summer fabrics. Their colorful outfits delightfully mirrored the natural beauty of these girls, contrasting perfectly with their wavy brown hair, fair skin, and deep, dark eyes. Without a pinch of makeup on their faces, their almond-shaped eyes reflected innocence, purity, and piety—the perfect image of a traditional Baloch girl.

Among each other, the girls spoke a language I could not identify. It did not sound like Balochi but more like Sindhi and

I could understand a few words. Later, I learned that they were speaking Lasi, the language of Lasbela. Considered a dialect of Sindhi by some, Lasi is primarily spoken by those native to Lasbela, many of whom have their roots in the neighboring Sindh. I had learned about the diversity of the region during previous visits, when I met many Hindus who migrated from the Thar Desert of Sindh, closer to their holy sites in Lasbela. When Jalal took me to the famous Hindu pilgrimage sites of the Chandragup mud volcanoes and the Hinglaj Mata Mandir, which attracts thousands of Hindu pilgrims from around the world, he praised the religious harmony in the region: "In Lasbela, we Muslims live side by side with our Hindu brothers. We shake hands and eat from the same plates; they truly are our brothers."

When it came to caste however, Jalal insisted: "Our family is Baloch and descended from the noble Rind tribe. *Alhamdulillah*, we Baloch are a very respectful, tolerant, and honorable people."

While the girls chatted with each other in Lasi, I was relieved to find out that most of them spoke English, a rarity in Lasbela. Fatima, the eldest daughter, spoke even better English than her father and we were able to communicate smoothly. Despite English being widely spoken in Pakistan, opportunities to hone one's language skills are rare in places like Lasbela, where foreigners are not usually allowed to visit. This was the first time the girls were able to practice their English outside of a school setting, which made their smooth communication skills even more admirable. In exchange, the girls taught me plenty of Balochi and Sindhi phrases that they deemed useful for my trip, such as "what is your caste?" and "where is your ancestral land?" Multilingualism is very widespread in Balochistan, with many

Baloch people speaking several languages. As a passionate polyglot myself, I felt I had found a great community.

Meanwhile, Jalal's wife repeatedly stepped in and out of the room to serve us everything from spiced milk tea to colorful sweets to a delicious lunch consisting of five different dishes. Every time, she entered with a full tray and left with an empty one. She was so inconspicuous that I did not even notice her until a delicious smell tickled my nostrils. One of the daughters spread out a plastic tablecloth on the carpet next to the *takya* on which her mother placed the food. We girls quickly gathered on the floor, ready to indulge in the delicious medley of colorful chicken and vegetable curries and lentils, served with fresh rice and *naan*. Although these dishes are staples in nearly every Pakistani household, their spices and textures vary every time, making every meal unique. Jalal's wife seemed to have added more black pepper than most people, giving the dishes a particularly piquant, piney taste. I enjoyed it a lot. After we finished our meal, two younger nieces cleaned up the floor within seconds by carrying the dirty dishes to the kitchen for their aunt to clean and folded up the plastic tablecloth, leaving not a single grain of rice behind. Of course, as their guest, I was not allowed to move a finger.

We had all retreated to the large bed on the other side of the room when Fatima turned towards me and excitedly asked, "Tonight, a girl from our neighborhood is getting married. Do you want to attend the wedding?"

Intrigued by the opportunity to witness a Balochi wedding, I felt overjoyed and accepted the invitation immediately. However, I had one major concern.

"I'm traveling with nothing but a suitcase full of everyday clothes. What should I wear for this special occasion?" I worriedly asked.

"Don't worry, you can wear any one of our dresses and use whatever jewelry you can find in this room," she assured me.

After digging through her full yet neatly organized closet for a good five minutes, comparing dress after dress, she eventually handed me her finest outfit, a black Balochi suit with multi-colored embroidery and mirrorwork. Along with it, she gave me a pair of earrings, a brooch, and a heart-shaped purple watch from her jewelry drawer. I was afraid the dress would be too large for me as was always the case when I tried on my friends' clothes in the cities, but surprisingly, it wrapped perfectly around my frail little body.

We girls spent the next three hours experimenting with whatever cosmetics we could find in the room. While one younger niece was stuck in a perpetual cycle of applying heavy, bridal-style makeup on my face, washing it off, and then reapplying it, the eldest daughter painted intricate flower patterns on my hands using high-quality henna paste. One girl skillfully arranged my lifeless, straw-like hair into gorgeous braids, just like my grandmother used to do, while others were busy searching for matching perfume and nail polish. In the meantime, numerous aunts paid visits to our room to exchange greetings, drink tea, and leave behind mountains of gifts for the guest—a common occurrence in Baloch households, the girls told me.

In the end, I barely recognized myself in the mirror: elegant dress, flawless hair, and a timeless makeup look resembling that of a Baloch bride—a divinely feminine version of myself I had no idea existed. Likewise, the girls of the family had also transformed themselves into gracious, bride-like ladies.

In awe of this impressive transformation, I instinctively pulled out my phone as the eight of us were standing in front of the mirror and exclaimed, "Let's take a group selfie!"

Considering the fact that I was surrounded by a bunch of gorgeous teenage girls, one might have expected a cascade of duckfaces, bunny ears, and peace signs. The girls, however, shrieked in horror and immediately buried their gorgeously polished visages into their fine head scarves. "Please don't capture our photos," they begged me in unison. "We're not allowed to have our photos taken. If our father finds out, he will never forgive us!"

Taken aback, I tried to investigate what the root of the problem was. I explained I had no plans to post the photos online or show them to anyone; I merely wanted a reminder of this memorable evening. But the girls were adamant: "Please don't take any of our photos with your phone."

Nisa, Jalal's youngest daughter, desperately implored, "You never know what happens with the photos on someone else's device. What if, God forbid, our photos are leaked, and strangers get to see our faces?"

"It's not that we don't trust you," Fatima clarified. "It's just too much of a risk for us." Instead, the girls offered to take my photo in front of the family's cars. They seemed to enjoy switching angles, experimenting with flash and filters, and spinning my body into many glamorous poses, as if this little photoshoot brought out the fashion photographer in every single one of them.

A sudden "Let's go!" was heard from across the garage as the others were busy draping my scarves and jewelry into the most aesthetic arrangements. It was the eldest niece.

"The wedding is about to start any minute. Let's not be late!" she urged.

———··•··———

Like an ensemble of Disney princesses, we made our way off the property, tightly holding onto each other's freshly manicured hands like a baby grabbing its mother's finger. We followed a sandy, unlit path along the house, gradually approaching the loud beats coming from somewhere down the block. Dismayed, I glanced at my favorite black sandals, which became covered in more dust with every step. Meanwhile, the girls seemed more concerned with covering their faces when an occasional young man passed by. No more than three minutes later, we reached the source of the loud music: a home.

Excitement overcame me as I followed the girls towards the narrow left-side entrance of the house, which was covered with an opaque curtain. I had attended a good handful of weddings in Lahore and Karachi, all of which featured a doll-like melancholic bride in a red dress sitting on an elevated stage inside a wedding hall, while large numbers of guests were spread across neatly arranged tables gossiping and indulging in copious amounts of rice and kebab. However, I had never been to a Balochi wedding and didn't know what to expect from a celebration held at home. My male Baloch friends had shown me videos of wild celebrations with men dancing and firing air shots, which made me very curious. This traditional small-town ceremony could only be more fun than the cookie-cutter weddings one finds in Pakistani cities.

With high expectations, I snuck behind the curtain, looking forward to what might be the most interesting wedding experience of my life. Immediately, I found myself in a spacious front yard surrounded by women of all ages sitting across the floor with wooden hookahs, called *chillim*, in their hands. Every single one of them was clad in fine *dooch*, turning the yard into a rainbow of colorful fabrics and stitches. There was not a single face without makeup in the hall, from dark kohl around infants' eyes to faces covered so thickly in white powder they resembled a white woman more than a Baloch. Loud folk music with fast beats was blasting from an old-fashioned speaker in front of the house, although nobody was dancing. Across the yard, there was not the slightest trace of a bride in sight. Assuming the ceremony had not started yet, I joined Jalal's daughters and nieces in a circle on the floor and pretended to participate in their gossip.

"This is our cousin from Karachi. She doesn't speak Lasi or Balochi," I overheard Fatima introduce me to another girl. The girl joined our circle and sat down next to me to strike up a conversation in Urdu. I tried my best to keep up but as my ears were flooded with unknown phrases and vocabulary, I began to stutter. Noticing my struggle, Fatima quickly intervened by saying, "She studies in London and struggles with Urdu sometimes." She then whispered into my ear: "Don't tell anyone you're a foreigner here and don't speak English. People here will talk bad about us if they know we hang out with strangers."

If there was one thing I learned in the hour of sitting on the floor with the girls, it was that reputation means everything for the women of Lasbela. From the teenagers in our circle to the aunties in the back, everyone was zealously watching each other's every move and there seemed to be not a single group that was not engaged in a passionate round of gossip. In fact, if gossiping were a sport, the women of Lasbela would be clad in trophies and gold medals.

"Look at that woman over there, she's such a monkey!" Nisa exclaimed while gesturing towards an older woman in front of us.

"What do you mean by 'monkey'?" I asked.

"Just look at her!" she urged me while pulling on my sleeve.

Indeed, the woman in front of us looked a little peculiar. She was wearing a pink dress with long, bright-red manicured nails, golden bleached hair, and light-blue contact lenses, and most discernibly of all, thick layers of porcelain-white foundation that covered her face like whipped cream.

"This is what a monkey looks like," Nisa explained in the tone of an old professor.

"Women like this are not good. They always want to be in the spotlight and show off," she added.

Of course, our group was not spared from the gossip either. As we were sitting on the floor listening to music, there was one very fast-paced Balochi dance song that caught my intention. According to the girls, the song title, which translated to "magic," was a favorite at Balochi weddings. To no surprise, the magic also worked on me and I could not help but snap my hands to the lively beats.

"Come on, let's dance!" the girls urged me.

I excitedly agreed and got up from the floor. Finally, my body was free to move to the beats that had captivated me so much. The girls asked the DJ to play the song from the beginning and our group assembled on foot in a small circle. Being unfamiliar with the local style of dance, I carefully followed all the girls' moves. They were very simple. We were walking step by step in our small circle and moving our hands outward to the fast beat. It felt impossible to keep my hips still while dancing, although I was cautious enough to keep my movements very limited. After all, we were in Balochistan, not Latin America. For the first time since arriving at the wedding,

I was enjoying myself. *Now the fun has finally started*, I thought to myself, when suddenly, barely twenty seconds into the dance, a voice yelled from the back, "Stop, stop! Sit down; quickly, sit down!"

It was Fatima, who had remained sitting and watching while we were dancing. "People here are laughing at you, quickly sit down before it gets worse!" she urged us. Then, she apologized to me: "I'm so sorry you can't dance here because the people are not good. All they care about is gossiping and they are watching out for every little detail to badmouth us."

Disappointed but understanding, I sat down in the circle with the other girls and we continued to listen to the fast-paced Balochi dance music with our bodies stiff as corpses. The fun was very short-lived. "Don't worry," Fatima promised me. "We are keeping track of all the songs you like and when we get home we can dance as much as we want."

Minutes felt like hours passing while we sat on the floor, still waiting for some sort of official ceremony to begin. "Let's have a look at the bride!" one niece suggested. *Finally, there is something to see*, I thought as I got up and followed the group of girls inside the house.

The house was a simple family home with its doors wide open. We passed through a series of empty rooms until we reached the last door frame, which was covered with an opaque curtain. Like the girls before me, I snuck behind the curtain to see what was there. In a small, heavily decorated room sat the bride. A young woman who looked to be in her early twenties, she was clad in colorful *dooch* with heavy gold jewelry and a scarf covering her face. Her sleeves were pulled all the way up to her shoulders and two women next to her were painting intricate henna designs on each of her arms. As in all the weddings I had attended, I could hear the bride sobbing uncontrollably underneath her scarf, and the other two women didn't look too amused either. There was no greeting, just a quick glance, and the girls and I left. "Today is the *mehndi* ceremony. The *nikkah* will be held tomorrow," the girls explained to me.

Like most Pakistani weddings, this celebration consisted of various functions spread across multiple days. During the *mehndi*, the bride's hands and feet would be painted with henna, a natural dye that remains on the skin for about a week. The *mehndi* is followed by the *nikkah*, during which the Islamic marriage contract would be signed and the bride would see the groom for the first time (keep in mind, marriages are usually arranged by the families and it is not rare for the couple to have never met each other before). Afterwards, the bride is ceremoniously bid farewell by her family and moves in with her husband and his family. Depending on the family, further receptions may be held before and after these main functions.

"So, will there be any more activities tonight?" I impatiently inquired.

"No, no, everything is taking place in private behind this curtain," Fatima explained. "For us, there is just the party outside with the music."

Once again, our group was in the front yard and gathered in a circle on the floor. And once again, the girls started gossiping, which was really the only thing to do at this wedding. "I really love these weddings! They are so fun!" one niece happily exclaimed, while the other girls nodded in agreement. I too nodded and tried to fake a smile. In reality, I was not enjoying the wedding at all. I had spent all evening getting ready for this event just to sit on the floor for hours and listen to gossip in a language I barely understood. It was torture not to be able to dance to the rhythmic music that played in the background as we were not allowed to move.

"We are so lucky to be here!" Fatima explained. "Normally, our father doesn't allow us to go to these weddings because the people here are not good. But because you are here as our guest, he made an exception."

The awkward smile remained frozen on my face. I tried very hard to hide my disappointment at this wedding that the girls had so proudly invited me to, but I was struggling. I could not even distract myself with my phone because the girls would get worried if I accidentally pointed my phone camera towards them. There was no way I could even take photos of myself because there would always be women in the background. In fact, the only footage I was able to capture of the wedding was a short video clip featuring nothing but our feet and the "magic" song playing in the background. The women's hall at this wedding was a strictly camera-free zone.

Recognizing the boredom in my eyes, Nisa shot me a compassionate smile and asked, "Aren't you traveling to Gwadar tomorrow? If so, you will need to wake up early and be well rested. It's better if we go home now." She was very obviously getting bored herself and wanted me to convince the others to leave.

"No, please let's stay a bit longer! We're having so much fun!" the other girls protested.

"But she's traveling! Rest is more important for her," Nisa argued.

Suddenly, seven pairs of puppy eyes were looking in my direction.

"What do you think, Bela?" the girls asked. "Should we stay, or should we leave?"

It was a tough decision. *Yes, for God's sake, please let's leave!* I thought to myself, but looking into the girls' hopeful eyes, could I really be so selfish and take their only fun away?

Eventually, I came to a compromise and announced: "Let's stay here for another twenty minutes, and then we can go home." Needless to say, those last twenty minutes felt like eternity to me.

The following morning, I woke up in the middle of the king-sized bed surrounded by three of the girls and four more girls who were sharing a mattress on the floor next to the *takya*. They were already awake but remained quiet so as not to wake me up. It was not late, but unlike Karachiites, the people of Lasbela tend to be early birds. Within a minute of opening my eyes, Jalal's wife came to our room with a tray of tea, and shortly after, the plastic tablecloth was spread neatly across the carpet, ready for breakfast to be served.

"Our father told us you will leave for Gwadar in the afternoon. Be ready to leave at three o'clock," Fatima announced.

This left us with plenty of time. As soon as we had finished eating our breakfast, one of the nieces began braiding my hair, while another one took out her palette and applied makeup to my face.

"You looked amazing in my dress last night. Therefore, I have decided to gift it to you," Fatima declared.

"I also noticed your kohl eyeliner made your eyes tear. Take mine, it's of better quality," Nisa added.

Before I could grasp what was happening, I was overwhelmed with presents. I gave my best try at *taarof*, the Iranian etiquette of rejecting each gift multiple times, but to no avail. The girls had already neatly folded all their presents and squeezed them into my suitcase. Hospitality in Balochistan is no joke!

"Remember we promised that we would dance at home?" Fatima asked. "Now is the time!"

Within seconds we had assembled into a small circle as we had at the wedding. Nisa locked the door to the room, then opened the music app on her phone and searched for "Balochi wedding songs." She turned up the volume to maximum and, soon after, we found ourselves once again moving in circles with small ballerina steps, elegantly flapping our arms outward to the fast beats of the song. This time, there was nobody to watch us, gossip, laugh about us, and interfere with our fun. We completely enjoyed ourselves and did not stop dancing until our heavy dresses were completely soaked in sweat.

Following our little girls-only house party, we still had a couple of hours left before my planned departure.

"What's your plan now? Is there anything else you want to do before leaving Lasbela?" Fatima asked me.

Looking at the wardrobe full of *pashk*, I could not ignore the desire to shop for my own clothing.

"Is there any market in Lasbela where we can shop for ladies' dresses?" I inquired.

With a slightly uncomfortable look, Fatima replied, "Yes, there is . . . but we never go there."

Confused, I wondered, "Then where do you get all your beautiful *pashk* from?"

"They're all handmade," she replied. "All our clothes are made by our mothers or aunts or even ourselves."

"I don't know if the market sells such dresses but if you want to go there you should ask our father," Nisa added.

Impressed, I compared the girls' dresses to my own. I had bought mine from the wholesale textile market in Karachi at a discounted price, machine-embroidered and custom-tailored, ready to wear the following day. Hand-embroidered dresses, on the other hand, take months and months to stitch and can sell on the market for hundreds of dollars, although most women tend to keep their dresses for personal use. Undoubtedly, Balochi *dooch* is an admirable form of art, which, thanks to widespread traditions, is kept alive by most women.

Afterwards, Fatima pulled me aside and explained, "You know, our culture is very different from what you are used to in the city. For us Baloch people, honor is very important, and we all strive to live respectable lives."

She sipped on a hot cup of *chai* that her mother had just served and continued, "*Hijab* is very important in our religion. After age eleven or twelve, no man is allowed to see our faces, except for our father and brothers, and our future husband after marriage. We can only show our hands and eyes. So, after this age we usually don't leave the house anymore. That's why we don't know much about the markets in town."

It was my turn to take a sip. I interjected,, "Why can't you leave the house, though? Can't you just wear garments that cover your face, such as *niqab*?"

"Yes," she replied. "But staying at home is better. It's better for the afterlife."

I knew that *hijab*, or modesty, is an important value in Islam for both men and women. Muslims around the world interpret the rules around modesty differently and social customs and dress codes vary greatly from person to person. Not all Muslims believe in strict gender segregation in all aspects of life and full body cover for women. Rather, beliefs regarding modesty are heavily intertwined with local cultural values. I learned that in Balochistan, many people believe that strict *pardah* is necessary, meaning that women are completely hidden from strange men. While locals typically justify this custom in the name of religion, it is also a way to show respect to and protect women according to local traditions. Of course, not all Baloch families follow *pardah* this strictly and attitudes vary greatly between cities, towns, and villages, as well as across socioeconomic ranks.

After a few seconds of silence, Fatima went on, "We are not originally from Lasbela. My sisters and I were born and raised in Karachi and went to school in Lyari. However, once we grew older, my father decided to move to our ancestral land."

She took another sip and continued, "The people in Karachi are not good. They don't follow the traditions and their faith is not strong. There are many bad influences in the city. Life in Lasbela is much better and the people are more respectable. There are no bad influences. That's why our father decided to shift here. To protect his daughters from bad influences."

After this conversation, the girls and I continued to talk, laugh, and beautify ourselves within the realm of the room. A sleepover with a group of teenage girls was a welcome change from my usual solo female travel lifestyle in Pakistan. Normally, I find myself surrounded exclusively by men for weeks, as women are a rare sight in the travel scene. Being the only woman in a group of men is not easy. No matter how friendly a man is to me, I can never accept his kind acts for what they are. I constantly have to be on the lookout for red flags as even the simplest acts can be motivated by bad intentions. Even when I am around "trusted friends," I need to question their every look, word, or move, since no man can be trusted completely. My body runs in survival mode around the clock, even when I sleep, yet no matter how careful I am, bad things still happen. I get harassed, touched, insulted, and deliberately steered into dangerous situations simply for traveling, being alone, and being female. Therefore, it felt beyond refreshing to spend time around my own gender. For twenty-four hours, I was safe. I did not have to fear where the hands around me went or the questions they asked. I could laugh, dance, and exchange my heavy *chadar* for a light *dupatta.* There was no need to doubt anyone's intentions. The girls' room in Jalal's house had become like a fortress sheltering me from the evils of the outside world, where I could simply relax together with an energetic bunch of girls who reminded me of my old teenage self.

Yet, I could not help but feel as if the same fortress that sheltered me also began to imprison my free spirit. Sitting on the floor of the girls' room, I tried to imagine a life without traveling, socializing, or leaving the house, keeping my face secret from the world, and being invisible to the public. I failed every time. Perhaps I had gotten so used to the "bad influences" of the city that the "pure" life of Lasbela seemed unimaginable to me. Being a traveler, I could see every corner of the world but only ever scratch the surface. I could witness humanity everywhere but not understand it. I could experience lives but not live them. Jalal's daughters and nieces were just like me but vastly different at the same time; and while we were sitting and laughing within the same four walls, I noticed, we were truly worlds apart.

A knock on the door tore me out of my thoughts. It was Jalal's wife, carrying a heavy tray of food for lunch. Once again, her daughters and nieces hurried to help her by spreading out the cloth on the floor and arranging the dishes. When I sat down, my heart skipped a beat when I realized she had cooked *namkeen rosh* especially for me. Her daughters must have informed her of my inexplicable love for tender, lightly seasoned mutton. I wanted to give her a hug, but by the time I realized what it was, she had already disappeared into the kitchen again. Instead, I excitedly tore off a piece of *naan*, soaked it in the rich broth, and used it to separate a big chunk of meat from the bone. I poured the remaining broth over the plate of rice, and at the very end, I cracked open the bone and sucked out the marrow. Cooking truly is a love language and in this meal, I tasted the love of a woman I had never talked to.

By the time we had finished eating lunch, it was almost three o'clock. While I was getting dressed for the journey ahead, the girls neatly arranged all my belongings and gifts in my suitcase. When I came out of the shower, they explained to me in great detail where in the suitcase every single item was located. Then, it was time to exchange our contacts.

"Our father doesn't allow us to make accounts on social media but we secretly use our little brother's Instagram account to talk to people," Fatima explained.

I handed her my phone and let her follow the account of a nine-year-old boy filled with photos of cars and guns. She called over her brother with his smartphone to accept the follow request. Then she typed a short message from his account to help me remember the username.

"I really hope we will stay in touch," she said with a smile.

Then, her expression became more serious as she begged, "Please don't tell our father about this. He will get very angry at us."

The next knock on the door was Jalal. He was ready to leave. I handed him my luggage, which he then carried to his pickup truck. In the meantime, I hugged goodbye to all the women in the house: first, to the daughters and nieces, then to all the aunts who were there, and lastly, Jalal's wife, who was in the middle of doing the dishes. Leaving behind a mountain of dirty plates, cups, and bowls, she dropped her sponge, rinsed her soapy hands, and briefly stepped out of the kitchen so that I could finally give her the long, firm hug that she deserved. Then, she immediately went back into the kitchen and continued to work. Looking back at the waving hands and tears of the women, I realized I had perhaps witnessed the greatest culture shock of my life. The day spent with the girls of Lasbela passed quickly but left a lasting impression and, unbeknownst to me, set a precedent for the rest of the journey. I had imagined this trip to be different, but the extent of that difference truly left me in awe. Little did I know this was merely the beginning. I hastily waved back at the women one last time while my mind was already with the men. After a day spent at home with the teenagers of Lasbela, I was now looking forward to an exciting, fun drive that would be closer to the way of traveling I had been used to.

CHAPTER THREE

JUST LIKE A MAN

By the time I reached the pickup truck, the vehicle was already fully loaded with luggage, water bottles, and snacks, and its loud engine was roaring, all ready to depart. Jalal was waiting in the driver's seat while Sanaullah and Umair sat in the back. They offered the front seat to me since the road ahead of us was extraordinarily scenic and they wanted their guest to enjoy the best views. There were no guns in sight during this trip.

"How was the wedding last night?" Jalal asked as he backed out of the driveway.

"It was great," I lied.

He smiled and replied, "I'm glad you enjoyed it. Normally I don't allow my daughters to go to these weddings. The people there are not good."

As we turned onto the main road, he reminded me to cover my face.

"Everyone in town thinks you're my family. Please put on your mask for now, otherwise people will think badly about my family."

By afternoon, the outside temperature was well above 40°C and the air-conditioning required some time to cool down the vehicle efficiently. Sweat was dripping down my face and the last thing I wanted to do was cover my face. Jalal however assured me that as soon as we left the town, I could take off my mask. The road we were going to travel on is typically empty and passes through few towns and villages, so there would be no people who could speak badly of us.

Once again, we passed smoothly through Lasbela's commercial center, leaving behind street vendors and butcher shops, auto repair businesses and barbershops, rickshaws and motorcycles.

We drove past the bus stop where the van had dropped me off the day before, after which the traffic thinned out and we left the town alongside colorful trucks and local buses.

As the air inside the car gradually became cooler and cooler, the sweat trapped inside the stitches of my *dooch* quickly evaporated and I finally felt relief under my mask. Refreshed, I looked outside of the window into the crowded buses that were rambling in the lanes next to us. Although their outsides were embellished with colorful painting, metal chains, and mirrors, the insides of these buses were anything but comfortable. and anyone who could do otherwise would have avoided traveling in them. Like the van I had taken to Lasbela, these buses were packed with men, women, and children squeezed tightly into the hard wooden seats, while their loading areas held everything from bags of rice and potatoes to live goats and chickens. As our truck overtook one local bus after another, I could only feel blessed for the comfort of my transport.

South of Lasbela we drove past dried-out lakes and fields surrounded by small mud-house settlements, military check posts, and more camels than humans. This landscape continued until a small yellow statue appeared at the end of the road— a miniature of the Princess of Hope, the most famous rock formation found in Hingol National Park, which we were slowly approaching. It marks the Winder Zero Point, the intersection where the Hub-Quetta Road branches off into the Makran Coastal Highway. Also known as the N-10, the highway is relatively new and smoothly links the coastal areas of Balochistan on the Pakistani side all the way to the Iran border. At roughly 600-kilometer-long, it was completed in 2004, drastically reducing the travel time from Karachi to Gwadar from nearly thirty hours to eight hours. In addition to connecting Pakistan's two major port cities, local settlements, and tourist resorts, the Makran Coastal Highway offers breathtaking views of Balochistan's Makran Coast and the rock formations of Hingol National Park. In my humble opinion, the Makran Coastal Highway is among the world's most spectacular roads and traveling on it is a pleasure.

Soon after merging onto the highway, the landscape flattened out and turned into a dried-out mud land scattered with desert scrubs. In the background, the rugged Makran Mountains began to reveal themselves. The only contrast in color to the white environment was the occasional colorful bright-orange truck. Most had faces painted on the back door, presumably depicting the trucks' owners. My mobile reception became weaker and weaker and eventually vanished completely. A quick glance at my offline maps revealed we had officially entered Hingol National Park.

Hingol National Park is Pakistan's largest national park and arguably the most beautiful. Characterized by distinctively shaped mountains, cliffs, sandy beaches, mud volcanoes, and green oases, Hingol offers a landscape equal to none. The exquisite formations of the Makran Mountains, which were created through erosion by the Arabian Sea's splashing waves throughout the land's history, appear to be sculpted by hand. People have even described the landscape as "Martian," implying it is otherworldly. Hingol National Park is a place where wildlife is bountiful, but humans are few. Although, over the years, more and more tourists have sought to witness this extraordinary landscape, many parts of it have yet to be seen by mankind.

At some unknown point on the road, Jalal turned left and drove off-road onto dried-out mud. The pickup truck glided over the wide cracks of the terrain, flattening all the scrubs that were in our way. A few kilometers in, the topography transitioned into tall dunes of yellow sand that made driving significantly harder. I joked that I hadn't signed up for a desert safari after our car nearly got stuck a couple of times. Jalal, however, did not seem to worry at all and even let Umair take over the wheel at one point. At age eleven, Umair's driving skills were truly impressive!

"What are we doing off-road?" I asked, confused.

"I want to refuel my car," Jalal explained.

A few minutes later, we reached a small industrial plant surrounded by tall dunes. Dump trucks would occasionally drive by, drop off tons of golden sand, and then leave loaded with black sand. I realized we were at the same sand-filtration plant I had visited during my previous trip. Last time, I had spent a night camping at the abandoned private beach from which the plant sourced its sand, which it then filtered for its metal-rich black traces. I had curiously explored the entire plant, witnessing the entire process from beginning to end. This time, however, we only stopped there for a short time. I took advantage of the opportunity to use one of the few washrooms we would encounter on our journey while Jalal refueled his truck.

Before I could climb out of my seat, he stopped me and said, "Wait a minute, let me take a look to check if there are any washrooms for ladies."

Of course, there were no specified ladies' washrooms in an industrial plant where only men work. He was rather referring to clean washrooms, as he would not want to offer a dirty washroom to a woman.

After a minute, Jalal returned and said, "The very last washroom is clean, so you can use it. However, you should take

Sanaullah with you because there are Pashtuns nearby. Those people don't respect women the way we Baloch do."

Without a word, Sanaullah followed me to the washroom, waited in front of the door until I was done, and escorted me back to the car. The washrooms were just around the corner and within sight of the vehicle, but Jalal would not let me go there by myself. He really seemed to distrust men of other castes and ethnicities.

When we got back to the car, I noticed Umair was missing. I looked around and suddenly heard an impudent "Hello!" As I looked up, Umair cheekily waved at me from the top of a sand dune. Without hesitating, I ran up the dune, dragging my heavy *pashk* through the golden sand until I fell. The dunes were soft as pillows and the sand fine as powder. I lay down in my natural miracle bed for a second then rolled down the dune like a child. All the while, Sanaullah held onto my phone and snapped hilarious photos of me. Strangely, I felt that in less than five minutes of this goofy play I had significantly more fun than I'd had during the entire wedding the previous night.

Umair and I tried to brush the sand off our clothes before getting back into the car, but too many of the tiny grains had become stuck in my fine embroidery. Luckily, Jalal did not seem to mind. His car was relatively neat and tidy but far from the impeccable cleanliness of his daughters' room.

When Jalal started the engine and hit the accelerator, the wheels began spinning, but instead of moving the vehicle forward, they only dug themselves deeper and deeper into the sand. Outside of the windows I could see mini sandstorms emanating from all four wheels. We had gotten stuck! Without a word, Sanaullah jumped out of the car to push it forward from the back, while Jalal continued to press the gas pedal. I also wanted to get out and help push but the men urged me to stay put and let Sanaullah do the work. Fortunately, he was able to push the pickup truck forward and free the wheels very quickly. Shortly after, we were on our way back to the main road.

"I've been lifting weights for three years, but I could never dream of singlehandedly moving a pickup truck the way you did!" I praised Sanaullah's strength.

"This is all thanks to Sanaullah's energy bars," Jalal replied, pointing to an open aluminum wrapper in the back seat.

"You should try some! It will make you very strong," he suggested while Sanaullah began to giggle.

Jalal took out a brown chunk from the wrapper and placed it in my mouth. Immediately, I wanted to vomit. The supposed "energy bar" had an intense bitter taste to it and a hard, woody texture that was impossible to chew. Jalal told me to keep it in my cheek for a few minutes and not swallow it. That was when I realized this was not an energy bar. All three were laughing at my grimaces as the pungent juice from the brown chunk pierced through every corner of my oral cavity. I lasted no more than a few minutes until the taste became so strong that I nearly puked the chunk out. It was disgusting! Jalal, Sanaullah, and Umair were still laughing as I repeatedly rinsed my mouth with water to get rid of the unpleasant taste, and I was still perplexed.

"This was not an energy bar," Jalal explained, trying to control his laughter. "It's *gutka*!"

Gutka is a type of chewing tobacco made from betel nut, tobacco, and other ingredients. It is immensely popular across South Asia despite being associated with various types of cancer and other ailments. When kept in one's mouth, *gutka* produces a pungent red substance that when spat out creates red stains that resemble blood stains. I had noticed Sanaullah spitting out of the window many times during the drive and now I finally knew the reason.

For the next ten minutes I felt horrible. My stomach was upset and migraines tortured my brain like they normally do before my menstrual period. As soon as the bitter aftertaste subsided, however, I experienced a strange craving for more. Before my brain could unmask the sneaky addictive scheme of *gutka*, I found myself asking Sanaullah for more.

However, Jalal noticed what was going on inside my head and called it quits. "No more *gutka* for you! This stuff is very bad for everything. Bad for your mouth, bad for your teeth, your throat, your stomach . . ."

Slightly disgruntled, I protested: "But Sanaullah chews it all the time! Why does he do it if it's so unhealthy?"

"It's very difficult," Sanaullah sighed. "All my guy friends were doing it and once you get hooked on it, it's impossible to quit."

Sanaullah's *gutka* addiction reminded me of the excessive *chillim* habits of many Baloch women I had met. I imagined that whether I were a man or a woman, I would certainly become addicted to nicotine in one way or another if I lived in Balochistan, and I was not sure if there was a lesser evil in this case. All tobacco products are highly addictive and carcinogenic, but many people depend on them to feel better and endure the physically and mentally stressful conditions of their everyday lives. I felt fortunate to have access to safe medications and live a comparatively easy life, and thanked Jalal for protecting me from a possible nicotine addiction.

We left behind the bumpy dirt path and returned to the highway for a short while, only to drive off-road again shortly after. This time, the path was just sandy, and the dunes were not nearly as high as in the previous spot. We drove along until we reached a small graveyard. Jalal turned off the engine and all four of us got out. We found ourselves standing in front of four large, ornate tombs surrounded by countless small heaps of stones. The tombs consisted of rectangular chests filled with beautiful pebbles and prominent, inscribed gravestones. They were all carved out of soft yellow-golden stone and contained intricate flower-like designs, similar to the famous Chaukhandi Tombs in Karachi. The graveyard was surrounded by smooth sand flats and on the horizon the turquoise sea was visible. A salty breeze entered our nostrils as we stood there and I realized we were at a beach.

"Over here, my parents and grandparents lie buried," Jalal explained, pointing at the four large tombs.

"I wanted to stop here for a minute to pay my respects."

I silently recited a prayer while simultaneously admiring the ornate tombs in front of me. I tried to imagine what Jalal's parents must have been like. Certainly, they must have had great honor to raise such a respectable son.

When he finished paying his respects, I inquired about the small heaps of stones next to his family's tombs.

"Those are the tombs of the commoners of our tribe," he explained. "Only my immediate family is buried in the big tombs because we are the leaders of our tribe." He exhaled deeply and then added, "My father got very sick before he passed away. It was painful to watch. I still miss him. He left us too early."

The difference between the tombs of the *sardars* and the commoners was yet another reminder of Balochistan's feudal society. The nobility's obsession with opulence and distinction from the masses does not end even at death. However, death spares no one. No amount of money or influence absolves one from the eventual fate of every soul and no ornamentation protects a body from decaying in the ground. We humans have created countless social constructs in this temporal world, but after death, nothing matters anymore.

On the way back to the highway, Jalal reflected out loud, "Umair is growing up so fast . . . now he is eleven years old. In five to seven years, I will have him get married so that he can continue our bloodline."

Taken aback and unsure of what to say, I eventually replied, "That's exciting! Have you chosen a girl for him yet?"

"Not yet," he answered.

"But for sure it will be someone from our family."

I silently did the math in my head: If Umair is eleven years old now, it means that he would be somewhere around sixteen to eighteen years when he gets married and starts a family. Being twenty-one myself, I could not imagine what it would be like to be in his shoes. At this point, I was just a carefree college student who spends her summers traveling the world. I was so uncertain about my own future; how could I possibly take on the responsibility of marriage and raising children at this point?

However, when I tried seeing the situation from Umair's perspective, the plan made more sense. He is Jalal's oldest son, making him the most important heir. Continuing the bloodline is a crucial responsibility in this position, and the sooner he gets married, the more time he will have to fulfill this duty. Unlike many of us, Umair was born into generational wealth and gets to skip the often decades-long process of working hard and saving up to support a family.

He does not need to go to university to earn a degree if his bloodline is his biggest qualification. Furthermore, in a traditional extended-family living arrangement there is plenty of support from older, more mature family members when it comes to raising children and managing a household. Well, that would be his wife's task, anyway.

As his father and I discussed his future, Umair seemed unbothered. He continued to scroll through his TikTok feed on his phone and occasionally exchanged funny videos with Sanaullah. He seemed to have full trust in his father and enjoy a worry-free childhood. Honestly, I felt a little bit jealous.

Cruising through the majestic natural beauty that is Hingol National Park, it was easy to forget about time. I looked out of the window to admire the golden sand dunes on my left, the rugged mountains on my right, and the smooth asphalt road sprinkled with colorful trucks and buses in front of us. These idyllic views were accompanied by a salty breeze entering through the car's vents and Kaifi Khalil's heartfelt Balochi music emanating from the Bluetooth speakers. I barely noticed how the sun's rays turned from yellow to golden to orange because the landscape looked equally gorgeous in every color.

After a while, the road became bumpier, and peaks began to emerge. I calmly waited because I knew the most splendid views were just ahead of us. And indeed, just another military check post and a sharp right-hand turn later there was a dramatic change in scenery as the turquoise water of the Arabian Sea revealed itself. We were now driving along an empty beach promenade, where large waves crashed against the smooth golden sand right alongside us. This spot has always been my favorite on the Makran Coastal Highway, and I look forward to it every time. Its name is Kund Malir.

Kund Malir is one of Balochistan's most touristic beach resorts and it is easy to see why. The clean, golden, fine-sand beaches and the warm turquoise waves of the Arabian Sea create the most beautiful contrast. Kund Malir is surrounded by tall white cliffs that offer ravishing views but the beach itself is smooth and easy to access. The water is neither too shallow nor too deep, currents are neither too strong nor too weak, and most of the time, the sea is safe for a myriad of water activities.

It came as no surprise that Jalal owned property in this prime location. During my last visit, he had hosted me and my companion in his private beach hut at Kund Malir. It was a simple but comfortable bungalow similar to his hunting lodges in the mountains. There was no air-conditioning, running water, or beds—only dusty carpets and *takya*. Certainly, it was no five-star accommodation but was convenient for spending a day at the beach. Jalal had access to a nearby garage with water skis, ATVs, and a small aircraft, and the tall sand dunes made Kund Malir an excellent spot to practice shooting, his favorite sport.

I silently wished we would stop here again this time and spend the night at his beach hut. Memories of swimming in the warm Arabian Sea in my long, flowy spandex burkini while little Umair and his father practiced air shots raced through my head. All I wanted to do was repeat them, relive them. To my disappointment, however, Jalal had no such plans. He said we needed to be in Gwadar the next day to prepare the paperwork for our crossing to Iran. I asked if we could stop at least for an hour to watch the sunset in this gorgeous spot, but he refused, explaining that we had to make it across Buzi Pass before the sunlight was gone. The next fifty kilometers on this road were going to be mountainous and full of sharp turns and Jalal was afraid to drive this segment in the dark.

I watched the large, turquoise waves splash against the golden sand as we drove by. We soon left Kund Malir behind and with the setting sun directly in the windshield, we began the drive through the hilly terrain.

Taking note of the disappointment in my eyes, Jalal comforted me. "Don't worry; Kund Malir is our second home. We can come here anytime, and you can swim as much as you like."

"We should also go hunting next time," Sanaullah added. "The mountains near our home are full of ibexes."

"That sounds great," I replied. "But my arms are so small I can barely hold a gun. How do you expect me to join you in the hunt?"

"No worries, we will teach you. If worse comes to worst, you can just join us for the *sajji*," Jalal assured me with a wink.

My mouth watered when I heard the word *sajji*. If there was one food I loved more than the salty boiled goodness of *namkeen rosh*, it had to be this zesty, well-spiced Balochi barbecue dish. Cooked to perfection over an open flame, *sajji* is the juiciest, most tender meat one could imagine. Still, I was skeptical that I could spend a day in the remote mountains surrounded by loud gunshots and blood splatter.

"We can teach you anything you want to learn," Jalal suggested. "If you want to learn how to drive, you can do so with my Land Rover."

"And I can teach you how to ride a motorcycle," Sanaullah added. "I love to go off-roading with my friends and then swim in a nearby pond."

Soon enough I was bombarded with a multitude of offers for my next trip. Whatever outdoor activity I was interested in, Jalal could arrange it. Completely free of cost for me, of course, since a Baloch would never let his guest pay a penny. It all sounded so exciting! I realized this was one of the rare opportunities of experiencing fun outdoor activities in Pakistan. I had always been told women can simply not do these things in Pakistan, but Jalal seemed completely different. He owned his own land where he made his own rules, and as long as there were no people around to judge, he was the most relaxed host in all of Pakistan. When I was with him and Sanaullah, I laughed, joked, and genuinely enjoyed my time, and I nearly forgot how strict he was to his daughters.

Right about when the sunset reached its climax, bursting with glorious colors, we passed by Hingol National Park's most legendary landmark: the Princess of Hope. This tall, human-shaped rock formation towered proudly over the mountains of Makran and resembled the silhouette of a woman staring out into the sea. Like all rock formations in Hingol National Park, the Princess of Hope is believed to have been naturally formed by the forces of wind and water, although some locals claim it is manmade. The Princess of Hope was given its name by none other than Angelina Jolie, one of the many visitors mesmerized by Balochistan's beauty. Most Pakistanis pride themselves with a global celebrity's attention to a landmark in Balochistan, but many of my Baloch friends believe the statue should have been given a Balochi name. Whether one is traveling by car, bus, truck, or motorcycle, the Princess of Hope is impossible to miss, not only because of its tall stature but also because of the road signs identifying it as a tourist attraction.

I convinced Jalal to stop at the Princess of Hope to take photos. Although I had already taken plenty of photos in this spot during previous trips, the pinkish-red tones of this late hour gave the scene a unique flavor. Jalal parked the pickup truck next to one of the road signs and before I could unbuckle my seat belt, Umair had already jumped out of the vehicle and ran excitedly towards the mountain. Energetically, he climbed up the rocks leading to the statue. I tried to follow him but in my heavy *pashk* and grip-less Balochi *sawas* sandals, I struggled. *Why do women's dresses always have to make everything so difficult*, I sighed, but then I remembered how gorgeous they look compared to Umair's t-shirt and jeans.

I gave my phone to Jalal so he could take photos of me. I was unsure what quality to expect because, after all, he never seemed to take photos of his own daughters. While I struggled to maintain steady poses on the porous, rocky terrain, he yelled commands in my direction: "Body towards me, face to the right, chin up, smile!"

Next, we took photos with the highway in the background. I looked out for cars and trucks on the road and then sat down on the warm asphalt. I lifted my *chadar* a little so that its embroidered mirrorwork reflected the last sun rays of the day and I pulled forward the thick braid that Nisa had woven my hair into. Both my *chadar* and my dress were bright orange and created a vibrant contrast under the warm evening sun.

The photos left me in awe. Each and every one was flawless in terms of angles, lighting, and even the poses Jalal had put me into. To my surprise, he turned out to be a gifted photographer and his mind seemed to work in the most creative ways. *How great it must be to have a hobby photographer as a father*, I thought to myself. Then I remembered that despite his obvious talent, he would never take photos of his own daughters.

Following our little photo shoot, Jalal was in a great hurry. The most difficult part of the road was yet ahead of us, and we had to cross it before the last sun rays disappeared beyond the horizon. Balancing both speed and caution, Jalal drove his massive vehicle up the increasingly steep curves of Hingol National Park's infamous Buzi Pass. The lines on his forehead grew tenser as the sky turned from magenta to lavender, and then indigo blue. From the comfort of my window, I admired the dramatic rock structures that made Buzi Pass a highlight of this drive. They were rising all around us like prehistoric staircases, and in the afterglow of the blue hour, they created an eerie yet oddly alluring atmosphere. Jalal, however, seemed hardly impressed by the mesmerizing landscape. He only went on to tell spine-chilling stories of trucks and passenger buses that fell to their demise along this part of the road. There was no way he could expose his guest to the risks of driving here in the dark.

To everyone's relief, the road flattened out just as the last glimmer of light departed from the sky. We had left Buzi Pass behind and, with it, the exciting landscapes of Hingol National Park. For the rest of our journey, the drive would be relatively uneventful, and I focused all my attention on Umair and his funny antics. We talked, laughed, and joked as our pickup truck smoothly cruised through the flat, dark void of Makran. There were no lights, no cars, and no people for miles, and the stars in the sky were the only aid to our vehicle's headlights.

We briefly stopped for a cup of *chai* in Ormara, the favorite beach resort of Karachi's youth. I listened to the soothing crashing of the waves from a traditional four-footed woven bed known as *charpai* as I sipped my cup of tea and wondered what the beach would look like in daylight. Was the sea still clean from the off-season or had it already been trashed by the busloads of city tourists that arrived here every summer weekend? Were the crabs still crawling in the sand or were they choking on all the plastic wrappers left behind? Were the locals happy?

"This *chai* is overpriced," Jalal grumbled. "In Lasbela I never pay more than ten rupees for a cup. Here they charge thirty!" He leaned in and lamented, "Ever since tourism has blown up in Ormara, the place has changed. The people have changed for the worse. I don't like Ormara. I prefer my land in Kund Malir."

On the long, dark drive after Ormara, I developed a runny nose. I tried to continue talking and joking but the tingling feeling in my nose made it difficult for me to enjoy the conversation. Noticing my frequent sneezes and teary eyes, concerned Jalal checked on me.

"Is there anything you need?" he asked.

"I need anti-allergy medication," I sighed.

Of course, I had no hope of finding a pharmacy along this empty road where even washrooms are rare, but before I knew it, Jalal had picked up his phone and made a call. All I could understand was "allergy" and "Pasni Zero Point."

About two hours after leaving behind Ormara and various check posts, we approached the small fishing town of Pasni in Gwadar District. I had the luck to visit Pasni during my previous trip to Balochistan and was immediately enchanted. Never before had I seen a sandy desert in sight of white cliffs surrounding the vast blue sea. Pasni's Juddi Beach is one of the most pristine of its kind; it houses the shrine of an "immortal saint" and is the main departure point for Hafth Talaar, Balochistan's largest offshore island. However, what fascinated me most about Pasni were its people. Nearly every person from Pasni I met was a gifted artist, and some of Balochistan's most talented photographers, filmmakers, painters, and poets were from the town. In fact, some people refer to Pasni as the "Lucknow of Balochistan," as it is the birthplace of innumerable poets. This comes as no surprise, considering Pasni's exceptional beauty leaves no mind uninspired, including mine.

The road remained pitch-dark as our vehicle came to a stop at a small intersection called Pasni Zero Point. Once again, Jalal pulled out his phone and made a call. A minute later I spotted a motorcycle pulling up next to us in the dark. As the rider approached, I recognized Usman, my private driver from my last visit to Pasni.

Usman was a man of his own kind. No older than age thirty, he had the demeanor of a retired fisherman. His life was simple and his attitude to it was equally easygoing. He seemed unable to spend a minute without laughing or giggling and could not even drive a meter without blasting cheerful Balochi music from his small car radio. His character was so full of glee that at times people would become suspicious of his intentions. He had driven me from Pasni to Kund Malir after showing me all around his hometown and inviting me to his family home but begged to accompany me all the way to Karachi. After convincing him otherwise, he nonetheless spent the night with us at Jalal's beach hut. The following morning, he asked for my contact number with the eyes of a middle schooler asking out his crush for a play date. As a woman, I had become all too familiar with this behavior. I did eventually share my number with him, but did not bother to save his, and brushed him off as a creep. After all, I imagined not *every* Baloch man respected women as much as a hundred weapons. Little did I know,

Usman would only call my number once, and only because his family missed me and wanted to talk to me.

Jalal rolled down the window and Usman greeted me with the most enthusiastic "*Asalamoaleikum, banuk! Chon e?*"

He engaged Jalal in a good ten minutes of loud small talk and awkward giggles while occasionally throwing wide smiles in my direction. It almost felt as if we were sitting in the middle of a *chai* shop, not a dark highway intersection. Time passed, and just as his conversation with Jalal came to an end, Usman handed me a brown paper bag. In it was a pack of small white tablets. Surprised, I thanked Usman and we exchanged our goodbyes.

As the young man rode his motorcycle off into the darkness, Jalal turned to me and said, "I told Usman about your allergy, and he came all the way to the highway intersection to meet us and give you anti-allergy pills from the pharmacy."

He added, "Usman may seem weird at times but at heart he is a very pure person."

And this was the impression I generally developed of the people of Balochistan, especially the common people who led simple lives. They lived in the most difficult conditions with a lack of pretty much everything a city dweller takes for granted: electricity, sanitation, healthcare, roads, infrastructure, safety, etc. I could count even more, yet they spread more kindness and positivity than most wealthy people do in their lifetime. I remember being received with warmth and hospitality by a family on the same day as one of their members passed away from a simple injury due to the lack of hospitals in the area. I have argued with *chai* vendors and rickshaw drivers in the poorest parts of town who did not want to charge me their fair wage, insisting that I was their guest. I have seen families living in houses without clean water and electricity feeding all the stray dogs in the village, whereas most city dwellers would have preferred to poison the animals they considered a nuisance. I have often passed by shopkeepers and security guards who laughed loudly for more than ten minutes at a time. I never knew the reason behind their glee, but it was contagious, and it elevated my mood more than *gutka* or *chillim* ever could.

As expected, the anti-allergy medication catapulted me into a deep sleep for the remainder of the journey. I woke up when the wheels of our pickup truck came to a smooth stop and the bright light in front of me forced my eyes open. We had arrived in Gwadar, and one of Jalal's acquaintances stood in front of our car to welcome us to his home. It was an imposing two-story building with all-white walls and ornate columns, protected by a grand gate that even the biggest of all pickup trucks could pass through. I sleepily stepped out of the vehicle and followed a servant straight to my assigned bedroom while another servant carefully rolled my suitcase across the smooth marble floor. I was to share my room with Umair while Jalal and Sanaullah would sleep in a separate room across the hallway.

As expected in a residence of such class, my room was opulently designed. There were framed paintings adorning the walls, expensive Persian carpets covering the floor, and grandiose chandeliers swinging above my head. However, it was not comfortable. There were air-conditioning units on the walls but due to power outages, these were not functioning, and the room was just as hot and humid as the rest of Gwadar in June. I tried taking a shower but only a few drops of water came out of the showerhead. Apparently, the building had run out of water and more would be supplied the next day. I tried charging my phone, but the unreliable power supply only left me worried for my device's battery health. Eventually, I decided to simply ignore the unbearable heat, swarms of mosquitos, and whatever other inconveniences I encountered in this lavish home and tried to get at least a few hours of sleep in before the men would come to wake us up in the morning. We had a busy day ahead of us.

The following morning was very hectic. After breakfast, Jalal, Sanaullah, Umair, and I spent the entire first half of the day driving from office to office to prepare the paperwork to enter Iran. Being from Balochistan, Jalal and his family were allowed to cross the border with merely a permission letter from the District Commissioner's Office in Gwadar. This document allowed them to visit specified cities for a specified purpose, and it did not give them permission to travel outside of Balochistan. I, on the other hand, had applied for an Iranian visa at the consulate in Karachi, which took longer to process but allowed me to travel across the entire country, as I had long dreamed of. Therefore, I spent most of the time waiting outside of the offices, bored.

Hours later, the men had finally completed their paperwork. Exhausted, Jalal informed me it would take three days for their permits to be processed due to a problem with the documents. The authorities in Gwadar had suggested he change his son's name on the documents as it sounded "too Sunni," which might cause him trouble with the authorities of the Shia-majority Islamic Republic of Iran. Until then, we would have to remain in Gwadar.

To be honest, I was not too disappointed by this news. After all, Gwadar was one of my favorite cities and there were plenty of breathtaking places to visit nearby. Passionately, the four of us began discussing which places we should visit during the next three days. A heated argument later, we eventually agreed to visit the marvelous sunset beaches of Jiwani the next day and spend the rest of this day exploring Gwadar.

Cruising along Gwadar's palm-lined Marine Drive was undoubtedly a delight, especially in the earlier half of the day when the sunlight projected a bright shimmer onto the turquoise sea, and colorful fishing boats returned to shore with their catch of the day. The seemingly only barrier between the perpetually aquamarine sea and sky were the characteristic white cliffs that tower over Gwadar from its hammerhead, a peninsula-like geographic feature that appears when washed-up sand links an island to the coast. These same cliffs gave rise to one of the world's most unique cricket grounds, although ironically, most natives of Gwadar were passionate football aficionados.

If asked to describe this city in one word, most people would choose "change" or "development." Oftentimes referred to as "the new Dubai," Gwadar was a mere fishing village, like most settlements along the Makran Coast, until a few years ago. Aware of the hamlet's ideal potential for hosting a deep-water seaport, however, China collaborated with the Pakistani government to realize this large-scale undertaking under the umbrella of the China Pakistan Economic Corridor (CPEC) initiative. Operated by the China Overseas Port Holding Company, the brand-new Gwadar deep-water port provided China with convenient access to the Arabian Sea as goods could be transported directly from the China-Pakistan border in the Karakoram Mountains through the diplomatically friendly country of Pakistan. In response to this large-scale project, Gwadar has experienced fast-paced development over just a few years, attracting everything from new businesses to posh housing schemes. While the city somewhat resembled a construction site at this point, many believed in a futuristic transformation for Gwadar.

However, if I were to describe Gwadar in one word, it would be "inequality." The city is clearly divided into two different worlds. On the one hand, there is the hammerhead, which, in addition to the CPEC port, houses luxurious five-star hotels. These posh hotels allow guests to indulge in poolside ocean views and fine dining at twenty times the cost of a regular meal in the area. Driving along the hammerhead by car, one could set aside all of one's worries and enjoy the refreshing breeze from one of the many parks and viewpoints. On the other hand, there is the mainland with the local settlements that resemble any other place along the Makran Coast: constant water shortages, incessant power cuts, and rampant public health concerns due to poor sanitation. The streets of the mainland are full of women beggars who, unlike the women of Jalal's family, cannot afford to stay home when the babies in their arms are crying from hunger. Gwadar's fast-paced development might attract rich investors and tourists from Karachi but how do the natives benefit when they can no longer put fish on the table due to overfishing à la trawler method? What do they get to see of their city's gorgeous white-cliff viewpoints when the check post at the entrance of the hammerhead turns them away for not possessing a special entrance pass?

Of course, Jalal decided to take his guest to the hammerhead, the "presentable" side of Gwadar, but his plans were shattered when the soldier at the check post waved us down and asked for our IDs and entrance pass.

"I don't have it on me," Jalal stuttered. "We just submitted our papers at the office today. I only have photocopies of our ID cards."

The officer did not accept any of the options that Jalal listed. No card, no entry.

"Please let us pass. I brought my family here all the way from Lasbela to admire the beauty of Gwadar. Don't you know who my father was?" Jalal begged.

The soldier did not want to hear any of the *sardar*'s pleas. He had a clear protocol to follow, which meant turning most people away. *Sardars* may have influence in tribal affairs, but in front of the official administration, they are just as powerless, no matter the size of their pickup truck.

"Forget about the hammerhead, just take me to the ladies' market," I tried to lighten the mood. After all, I was more interested in experiencing local life anyway.

"But we don't have any lady to accompany you. You'd be all alone out there," Jalal reasoned.

In a place like Balochistan, it came as little surprise that even the markets were gender separated so that women could shop for clothes and embroidery supplies without encountering men. However, being men, neither Jalal nor Sanaullah had ever set foot in a ladies' bazaar, hence they could only guess what visiting there would be like.

In an attempt to structure the remainder of the day, Jalal contacted person after person to ask for advice. That was, until he received a call from an unknown number, and without explanation, he ordered all of us to get in the car and he began driving.

Without saying a word, Jalal drove farther and farther. His expression stiffened, and he rarely lifted his foot off the gas pedal. I confusedly looked out of the window, realizing we had left behind Gwadar and were driving back eastward. There were road signs for Pasni, Ormara, and Karachi. Very clearly, we were not going to Jiwani. After passing Gwadar Airport, the road once again turned into vast nothingness, only white sand with a few rocks and shrubs sprinkled in between. *Where the heck were we headed?* I thought to myself.

A good half an hour later, we made a right-hand turn towards an area that looked familiar to me. I checked on the map and realized we were in Surbandar, a small town where I had briefly stopped on my last trip to Gwadar.

Jalal steered into a large property on the outskirts of town that quite resembled his own family home in Lasbela. He parked his large pickup truck next to a row of similar vehicles and all four of us got out. The man who welcomed us seemed familiar. When he greeted me by my name, I realized he was Imran, the man who had shown me around Gwadar during my last visit. He ushered the four of us into a small, hot, non-airconditioned one-room structure separate from the house. We settled on the characteristic red-yellow carpet next to a couple of *takya* and the men began conversing in Balochi. There was no cell reception, and all I could do was swipe through my phone gallery to admire the photos from the previous day. A few minutes later, a servant emerged from the house with a tray of *chai* and delivered it to our room. Sweat ran down my head in rivulets as I silently sipped on my cup of steaming hot-milk tea and tried to come up with millions of possible explanations for why we were here.

Seeing the boredom on my face, Imran turned to me and asked, "Do you want to meet my family?"

Jalal and Sanaullah exchanged encouraging nods, and I reluctantly agreed.

"You go with her," Jalal nudged his son.

Umair and I stood up and followed Imran to the house. Still, I had no clue what we were doing here.

Once inside the house, a group of three middle-aged women greeted us, including Imran's wife, Dur Bibi, whom I had also met during my previous visit.

"Good to see you again," Dur Bibi smiled as we exchanged hugs.

Belonging to a wealthy family, Dur Bibi represented the epitome of an elegant Baloch *banuk*, or lady. Clad in high-quality handmade *dooch* from head to toe, Dur Bibi was covered in copious amounts of gold jewelry. This included multiple solid gold rings and bangles on her hands, heavy necklaces and headdresses, prominent earrings and nose pins, and the characteristic Balochi *waleeg*: a collection of gold rings along the outside of the ear's cartilage, known as helix piercings in the West. *Waleeg* is typically worn by married Baloch women, with many girls getting their ears pierced as soon as they get married. Like the rest of the gold jewelry, most of these rings are either passed down from mother to daughter or gifted by the groom's family at the time of the wedding.

"How can you leave the house wearing all this expensive jewelry without getting robbed?" I once asked Dur Bibi, to which she replied, "In Gwadar I don't need to worry. Baloch men are very respectful and would never dare to rob a woman because they cannot touch strangers. However, when I go to Karachi I can't wear my bangles, rings, necklaces, and headdresses. I can only wear my *waleeg*, which is covered by my *chadar*."

One of the other ladies left the room to prepare *chillim*, while the other two engaged me in their small talk.

"This was us at a wedding last month," Dur Bibi presented photos on her phone.

In the photos, one could see the same three ladies wearing the same jewelry and similar dresses, in addition to heavy makeup and thick artificial unibrows. Swiping through the photos, I could not help but be fascinated by the vastly different beauty standards. Growing up in Germany, I used to desperately pluck my unibrow as I would be considered "unkempt," yet these women deliberately painted on their unibrows.

One photo on Dur Bibi's phone left me particularly startled. "How did you get a photo of me?!" I incredulously exclaimed.

Dur Bibi gave me a confused look. "What do you mean? This is my sister from Karachi," she murmured.

I gave the photo a closer look and realized it was a woman who had equally pale skin and dark hair and her facial structure was very similar to mine.

"You are right, though," Dur Bibi muttered. "My sister also has a perfect nose like you."

Once again, I was shocked. *Perfect nose?* I used to be bullied for my long aquiline nose and some people even suggested me to get a nose job to "fix" the noticeable hump on my bridge.

"Perhaps I should move to Balochistan so I can be beautiful," I joked.

Comparing beauty standards while puffing filter-less waterpipes was pleasant for the first half an hour, but not long after, I got bored—unlike Umair, who had been smart enough to download his favorite TikTok videos onto his phone. When the ladies eventually left for the kitchen to begin their dinner preparations, it was just me and Umair left in the room.

"What's the plan for this afternoon?" I asked him.

"No idea," the eleven-year-old replied.

"Are we going to the beach here in Surbandar?" I followed up.

"Ask my father," he replied.

I glanced outside, and to my surprise, I realized Jalal's pickup truck was gone.

Confused, I asked Umair, "Where did your father go?"

The boy gave his trademark answer of, "I don't know."

Time passed slowly. Exhausted after spending hours attempting to play with a child and disappointed that my Urdu skills were insufficient to carry on a conversation with someone half my age, I came to the bittersweet realization when I noticed it had gotten dark outside. On the one hand, I felt frustrated that I had wasted an entire day in one of the world's most beautiful places, sitting in a room trying to smoke away my confusion. On the other hand, I felt relieved that the day was almost over and soon I could go to sleep and do more exciting things in my dreams. Neither thought could beat my strongest emotion, which was concern. I had repeatedly tried calling both Jalal and Sanaullah throughout the afternoon, but their phones were powered off. I wanted to blame this on the abysmal network coverage in the area, but deep inside I felt that something else was going on. I had no clue what it was but guessed that it was nothing good.

After a while, I noticed bright lights flashing up in the dark front yard along with the sound of a massive engine. The men had finally arrived! Relief temporarily contained the thousands of questions that were running through my head, while the women frenziedly threw their scarves over their faces and hid in the closest room.

Excitedly, Umair and I ran outside into the yard to greet the men. However, when I saw Jalal's face, I noticed the lines on his forehead had become darker than ever and his eyes conveyed nothing but concern.

"Let's sit down there," he mumbled while pointing towards a set of plastic chairs in front of the building.

"I have bad news to share."

Jalal pulled out a chair, cleared his throat, and began the story: "Today after we came back from the offices, I received a call from an unknown number. The caller requested a private meeting . . . turns out it was the intelligence agencies calling. I don't know how they got my number or heard about us . . ."

Intelligence agencies? Even as a foreigner, I knew how unbelievably powerful this institution is in Pakistan, and a call from these guys would send chills down anyone's shoulders.

He tried to contain his shaky voice. "They yelled at us and spoke in a rude tone. Nobody has ever talked to me like this. I told them who my father was, but they didn't bother to listen . . . they just said we were in trouble."

"In trouble for what?" I impatiently interrupted.

Jalal took a deep breath and responded, "For taking a foreigner to Gwadar without permission."

My jaw dropped as I heard this.

"But . . ." I stuttered defensively, "my friend told me he had arranged my permission for this trip!"

"He told me the same thing," Jalal sighed.

"How is this possible?" I uttered in disbelief.

It did not come to my mind at the time that both of us had fallen for a pathological liar. My so-called friend, who claimed to have connections in the highest of all places, was nothing but a fraud. He not only lied about arranging my permission, which caused trouble for innocent men like Jalal and Sanaullah. He went on to do much, much worse things to me later on, but that would be a story for another book.

"So, what will happen next?" I meekly asked.

"Well, the agencies told us we can't travel any farther with you in our car. Not even returning to Karachi with you is an option. But they were also not willing to provide transportation for us . . . What do we do?" Jalal was visibly at a loss.

We realized that trouble had taken us by surprise and there seemed to be no way out. These two kind men who extended their help and hospitality to their foreigner friend, and I, a young woman who just wanted to travel to Iran by road, now found ourselves stuck in a stuffy small room in Surbandar, unable to go anywhere, and uncertain about our next destination. What could we possibly do?

For the rest of the evening, the atmosphere remained tense as we tried to think of a plan. Imran's call for dinner briefly interrupted our thoughts and we settled in the guest room, where the food had already been laid out. The dinner consisted of a dozen different fish, legume, and vegetable dishes spread out across a plastic tablecloth on the carpeted floor. It came as no surprise that it took the women hours to prepare such an elaborate and delicious meal. As the cherry on top, afterwards we were served a bowl of *kheer*, a sweet milk rice dessert seasoned generously with cardamom, nuts, and dried fruits.

As if this heavy meal had replenished their starved brains with energy, the men eventually calmed down and began to think strategically.

Finally, Jalal came up with a plan: "We will call you a taxi to the border tomorrow early in the morning. You will have to cross by yourself because our permits are not ready yet. My friend will pick you up across the border and take you to his home in Chabahar."

With no alternative, I nodded in agreement.

Then Jalal turned towards me and in a soft voice he said, "I'm really sorry to leave you alone and I'm worried about you. Baloch men are very respectful, but you can never trust the ones on the Iran side. Like the ones in Quetta and Oman, the Baloch in Iran can be a bit *tharki* (creepy) at times. I just hope your host will treat you right."

That night, Jalal decided we needed to go to sleep earlier than usual because my journey to Chabahar should be completed during daytime. The men claimed the border region would be dangerous after dark because the remote desert and mountains were a refuge for bandits and rebels.

Soon after dinner, Jalal asked me to shift to the main building, where Imran's family was sleeping. "Go with the women," he said.

Slightly annoyed, I gathered my belongings. I was enjoying my time with Jalal, Sanaullah, and little Umair, who by that time had become like brothers to me. Imran's family was friendly, but the men seemed more relatable, and I wished I could spend more time with them.

Just as I was ready to move to the main building, Jalal began thinking out loud. "The air-conditioning inside is not working and it will get very hot at night. Do you prefer to sleep outside with us?"

I felt surprised and conflicted by this offer. Yes, I did want to stay with the men, and sleeping under the open sky sounded exciting, but as a woman I also knew I could never be careful enough. Sleeping next to strangers of the opposite gender was completely against the local culture, and if a Baloch man made such an unusual offer, one could not be sure of his intentions.

Jalal stepped outside of the guest room and arranged the *charpai*. He lined up three of the simple wooden bed frames next to each other. The first one was for the *sardar* himself, the second for Sanaullah, and the third for Umair. Then, he pulled out a fourth and, with a generous gap in between, placed it next to Umair's.

"This one is for you, in case you decide to stay with us."

Without a word, I lifted the light blanket from the *charpai* and lay down. I made the unusual decision to spend the night outside with the men.

It was the middle of the night, and the sky was covered in millions of stars. In the vast darkness of Makran, these distant celestial bodies were the only source of illumination. My bare eyes were trying to identify all the constellations I had been taught in the books when a shooting star crossed my view of the mighty Milky Way. What a privilege it was to sleep under this divine display of omnipotence! I closed my eyes and listened to the faraway sounds of waves and sea birds when suddenly a voice emerged. Mobile connection had returned for a brief moment, and Jalal used this opportunity to send a voice message to his friend: "You won't believe it but it doesn't feel like I'm traveling with family at all," I overheard him whisper in Urdu. "She's just like a man!"

I silently giggled at this remark. I had been told by Pakistanis that I "walked like a man" due to my fast pace—ladies should walk more elegantly, slowly, with smaller steps and less vigor; or that I "traveled like a man" because I did not complain about the cleanliness of the hotels I stayed in; but this was my first time hearing that I was "just like a man." Part of me thought this was a funny thing to say about someone who suffered from a myriad of gynecological complaints every month, while another part of me thought, *Perhaps I'm really more man than woman.* I enjoyed outdoor activities more than makeup, had more fun in a pickup truck than at a wedding, and was now sleeping outside with the men rather than inside with the women. The sheltered lives of Jalal's daughters seemed beyond my imagination, yet I could totally see myself going on hunting and camping trips with Umair and Sanaullah. Clearly, something was wrong with me. Perhaps I was born into the wrong body?

I did not want to distract myself too much from the magic of the moment with these introspective tangents, so I tried to focus my senses on the beauty of nature around me. Tiredness soon overwhelmed me but I felt reluctant to close my eyes to the breathtaking skyscape above me. *Don't worry, this is only the first of many such nights to come*, I eventually tried to convince myself. From now on, I would continue to travel just like a man and repeat the fun experiences I shared with Jalal and Sanaullah hundreds of times over until the very last moment of my trip. At least that was what my ignorant self thought in that moment.

CHAPTER FOUR

BANUK BELA

Soft sun rays gently stroked my skin, and a salty breeze tickled my nose. It was early in the morning, too much so for a night owl like me.

"Wake up and get ready, the taxi is coming in twenty minutes" were the words with which Jalal pulled me out of my dreams.

I was tired but the adrenaline that was racing through my veins quickly brought me to my senses. Today, I would cross the Pakistan-Iran border all by myself and travel through an area that locals deemed dangerous. As if this thought was not already nerve-racking enough, the intelligence agencies had left us with no clear instructions, and I was not even sure if continuing my journey westward was the right thing to do. I felt my heart pumping so hard it sent shockwaves across my body, and my limbs could hardly control the tremble.

Soon after, the taxi arrived and the men rushed to load my bags onto the vehicle. Jalal sent Sanaullah to accompany me to the border. At least for that part I was not alone. Still, my anxiety was crippling me. Sanaullah and I climbed into the rusty vehicle and greeted the driver. He sat down in front while I sat in the backseat. Then, both of us locked our lips shut and threw the keys out into the dust—at least this was what it felt like.

It took about two hours to reach the border town of Gabd from Surbandar. To phrase it more accurately, Gabd is merely a tiny village, like all settlements between Gwadar and Chabahar. I spent the entirety of the drive staring out of the window, watching the lifeless clay desert inland of the coast. Every now and then, I inconspicuously patted my pocket for the four one-hundred-dollar bills in my wallet. This was all the money I had for my three-week journey since international bank cards were not accepted in Iran. I tried to message my host in Chabahar, but there was no mobile signal. Sanaullah, sitting in front of me, did not utter a single word.

Eventually, two huge flagpoles emerged from the monotone landscape. One was carrying the flag of Pakistan and the other of Iran. There were dozens of oil tankers parked in front of us, and the smell reminded me a bit of a petrol pump. We had finally reached the border!

Sanaullah and I got out of the car and he swiftly introduced me to the guards as his family member. He unloaded my bags and carried them through customs, while I went into the immigration booth to collect my Pakistan exit stamp.

"Do you speak Balochi?" was the first question the officer asked me.

"A bit, but Urdu is better," I replied, hopeless to find an English-speaking officer at this border.

"Where are you from?" he asked.

"Germany," I replied while handing him my red passport.

"I mean, where in Balochistan is your hometown?" he rephrased his question.

"My family is not from Balochistan," I insisted. "I'm German."

"I see," the officer mumbled. "So, what is your Baloch tribe?"

At this point, I had given up all hope of making the officer understand.

I briefly glanced at Sanaullah who was waiting with my bags outside of the booth, then I turned back to the officer and dryly replied, "Rind."

"How great," the officer replied and stamped my passport.

"Allah hafiz, *banuk*," he bid me farewell without asking any further questions.

Once I had cleared immigration, it was time to say goodbye to Sanaullah. He accompanied me right up to the border line, and then handed all my luggage to a group of men in front of me. Without hesitation, they carried my bags across the border, despite not having exchanged a word with me. All they knew was that I was crossing the border by myself, and letting a woman carry heavy bags would have been a disgrace.

Entering Iran was equally smooth. There was only a short stretch of no man's land and despite the crowds, the waiting time to enter the Iranian immigration booth was not long. Upon presenting my passport, the immigration officer asked few questions and stamped my visa page without further ado. But soon enough problems arose. After crossing the border, I had no cellular signal, and there was no way to contact my host. There were no cars and no buses to Chabahar, and all I could do was wait to get hold of an immigration officer who eventually lent me his phone to call my host. Meanwhile, the unbearable heat inside the sticky immigration booth caused my clothes to become soaked in sweat, and I nearly passed out from dehydration. There was one small cooler containing stale and odorous water for the hundreds of travelers who crossed. I picked up the stained, dusty plastic cup on top of the cooler, filled it to the brim with the murky water, and gulped it down all at once. At this point, the possibility of developing severe waterborne illness a few days later when I would be surrounded by a host family with access to medical care outweighed the risk of passing out while waiting in this sweltering office.

It was about two hours later that the same officer pulled me out of my delirium, although it was difficult to keep track of time on the brink of heatstroke.

"Come out. A car has arrived for you," he said in heavily accented Urdu.

I got up from my suitcase, which had served as a makeshift chair all this time, and passed it to the officer, who carried it to a black Toyota. I followed him. Inside the car were three men: one young man with tan skin, hazelnut hair, and bright green eyes, dressed in loose beige *shalwar kameez*; one sturdy middle-aged man—the driver—with charcoal hair, thick glasses, and blue eyes; and one elderly man, whose frail, darkly tanned body was covered from head to toe in loose white cloths. They gestured to me to sit in the front next to the driver. Without saying a word, he started the engine and we drove off into the barren flatlands. *Who are these men?* I asked myself. *Are they going to take me to my host family in Chabahar or did I get into the wrong car?*

A few minutes later, the driver stopped to drop off the elderly man at a seemingly random spot along the small, dusty road. The frail man thanked the driver and wandered off into the flats, where he joined a small herd of goats. This led me to the conclusion that I was traveling in a shared taxi that my host must have had arranged for me. Confident that the remaining two men were also strangers, I put in my earbuds, leaned back, and enjoyed the cool air coming out of the car's fans. *Finally, I can catch up on my desperately needed sleep*, I thought.

As soon as I closed my eyes, however, the driver nudged me. "Do you want something to eat?" he asked in Urdu.

"No thank you, I'm fine," I politely declined, despite the loud grumbles coming from my stomach.

"I'll have food ready for me when I reach Chabahar."

Perhaps the driver doesn't know I have a host family waiting for me, I thought. *If I eat something now, I will be full when I arrive in Chabahar.*

I put my earbuds back in, but the driver nudged me again.

This time, he introduced himself: "My name is Mureed and I'm your host from Chabahar. Behind me sits my nephew, Dawood. Jalal told us a lot about you. You're our guest and you will stay with my family."

My tired blank face quickly transformed into a polite smile, as I tried to conceal my confusion and embarrassment.

"Nice to meet you," I courteously replied.

I realized, from now on I could no longer sleep or listen to music. I was not in a shared taxi but indeed in the car of my hosts. I had to be friendly to them, no matter how awkward the first couple of minutes had been.

"Before we go to my home, we will visit Dawood's village on the way to have some tea," Mureed announced.

I watched the dry landscape for the remainder of the drive, in hopes of seeing something that would pique my interest, but to no avail. Every square kilometer was just as barren as the previous one, with a few rocks emerging from the desert every now and then. Rimdan, as the border crossing is known in Iran, lies a couple dozen kilometers inland of the coast, distant enough for the landscape to differ drastically from the spectacular views of the Arabian Sea. Nonetheless, I felt content. I had finally made it to Iran, a dream come true, although I was aware that, apart from political jurisdiction, little was different: I was still in Balochistan, around Baloch people with the same language and culture, and I expected to see few differences.

After passing one of the few towns along the main road, Mureed turned onto a bumpy, dust road. A few kilometers ahead, palm trees emerged from the dry landscape, and we passed by a small but clear pond. In the middle of this oasis was a cluster of mud houses decorated with freshly washed *pashk* of all colors drying in the sun. We had reached Dawood's village.

Like in Lasbela, dozens of women of all ages emerged from the houses and welcomed me with hugs and kisses on my cheek.

"*Asalamoaleikum banuk, bya*!" they gestured to me to come inside one of the rooms.

At first sight, the room appeared like any village home in Pakistan: a simple, clay-covered one-room structure without windows, only a small door for light, the floor covered with a large yellow-red carpet and takya. There were a couple of charpai in the back of the room, some of which had cloths bound under them to function as infant swings. The room was devoid of any unnecessary items but filled with women, children, babies, and laughter.

There was, however, one key difference to the village, town, and even city homes I had visited in Pakistan. I noticed it as soon as I set foot in the room: air-conditioning. Unlike in Pakistan, even the simplest room of this village home was equipped with a functional air-conditioner that cooled down the interior so effectively that entering the room felt like a mountain retreat. I was surprised.

"How come this air-conditioning functions so well? Doesn't the electricity cost a lot? What about load shedding?" I threw many questions at Dawood, the only man who had come inside with us, and the only person in the room who could speak Urdu.

"We don't have load shedding here. That only happens in Pakistan," he replied, nonchalantly.

"I spend half of the year in Pakistan, the other half in Iran," Dawood went on. "In Pakistan, we have electricity, water, and gas shortages all the time, but not here. This side of the border is comparatively well developed."

Still in awe of the functional air-conditioning, I reached out for the cup of *chai* in front of me, but to my surprise, its content was clear and red, unlike the milky brown *masala chai* I had known for all these years. It was Iranian *chai*, not Pakistani *chai*! *Perhaps there are more differences across the border than I expected*, I thought to myself.

As I sipped on my cup of plain black tea, I felt a tap on my shoulder. I turned around and next to me sat a girl roughly the same age as me. She looked gorgeous, with flawlessly soft caramel-colored skin, wavy black hair, and greenish-brown almond-shaped eyes, with long lashes and luscious lips. She pulled out a children's toy makeup kit, gestured towards her face with a tapping motion, and gave me a cheeky smile.

"She wants you to do her makeup," Dawood explained.

"This girl just got married a few days ago, so she likes to experiment with cosmetics."

I blushed upon hearing this and awkwardly replied, "I'm not good with makeup. I'm afraid I will not be able to do a good job."

The truth was not that my skills were subpar, but rather I was afraid I would not be able to produce good results with the low-quality makeup that I was to use. Besides, I thought I was done with these boring beautification shenanigans after all the time I spent with the men.

"Doesn't matter, just try it," Dawood encouraged me as the girl pulled on my sleeve.

I reluctantly agreed and reached for the face powder that the girl handed to me. The shade was porcelain, way too fair for her delicate golden-brown skin.

"This is the wrong shade. Are you sure you want to use this powder? You would look better without it," I asked Dawood to inform the girl, who gestured to apply it anyway.

I gently placed the powder sponge on her face, but every pat felt painful to me. Not long after, the girl looked like she had drowned in a birthday cake.

Afterwards, she handed me pitch-black eyebrow powder, dried-out liquid eyeliner, brittle eye shadow, and bright-red lipstick as smudgy as warm butter. I tried my best to give the newlywed a decent makeover, but there was little I could do with the limited resources. In the end, I felt ashamed to see that, under my stroke of the brush, this natural beauty came to look more like a clown from a horror movie than a bride.

"I'm sorry; I have difficulty using this makeup. The quality is not good," I apologized embarrassedly when I noticed the horror on the girl's face as she viewed herself in a hand mirror.

Without saying a word, she grabbed a tissue and thoroughly cleaned her face. Then, she took the brush into her own hands and applied the makeup herself.

Ten minutes later, I was shocked to see the girl had transformed herself into a stunning bride-like beauty, just as gorgeous as her natural self. She left me at a loss for words. *How is this even possible?* I wondered.

After I gathered myself from the surprise, I stuttered, "You look incredible! How did you do this?"

The girl answered with nothing but a sassy wink, but as the

other women took note of my embarrassment, they tried to console me. "It's okay, she just got married recently, but you aren't even married yet. How can you know any better?"

I tried to deflect from the makeup debacle and instead focused on the girl's beautiful *waleeg*: four large gold rings along each of her ears that were impossible to ignore. They seemed so heavy, yet they clad her ears gracefully, unlike my own helix piercings, which kept getting infected. *What's her secret, and how did she get it done?* I kept asking myself. Eventually, I asked her about her piercings.

"When did she get her ears pierced?" I inquired.

"About four days ago, when she got married," Dawood translated her response.

"Does it hurt a lot?" I followed up, recalling my own painful piercing experiences.

"Not at all, she says."

The girl's answers left me in shock. How was it possible to wear such heavy jewelry only a couple of days after piercing, and how did the wounds remain so clean?

Even more intrigued than before, I asked, "What technique do they use here to pierce ears?"

"First, we take an embroidery needle to pierce a hole through the ear and weave a thread through it. A few days later, we replace the thread with gold rings," and elder woman explained.

Then, she smiled at me and Dawood translated her words: "She's offering to do your *waleeg* as well. Do you want her to?"

An excited grin escaped my lips. I seriously considered this offer for an instant, but eventually I decided I was too intimidated by the thread and needle method, and too broke to afford so many gold rings.

"Thanks, but I'm not married yet," I politely declined.

"No worries; they say they will come to your wedding and do it then," Dawood replied.

Suddenly, he turned towards me, his eyes gleaming as he announced, "I'm getting married next year, *Insha'Allah*! You are cordially invited."

"That's great! Where is the wedding going to be?" I asked.

"Not sure yet, maybe in Turbat or maybe here," he answered.

"Please promise you will come, though," he insisted. "If you come to my wedding then we will all attend yours."

"I will try my best to make it," I awkwardly replied. "School is very stressful but *Insha'Allah* I will be able to join you."

I was not sure which prospect unsettled me more: attending another wedding like the one in Lasbela, organizing my own huge function that would accommodate entire villages, or getting my ear cartilage pierced with the thread and needle method. Therefore, I felt quite relieved when Mureed's voice sounded from outside the room, telling Dawood and me to get ready to leave for Chabahar.

I warmly reciprocated all the women's hugs and kisses as they wished me goodbye with a soft "*washi*." As I was about to leave, the newly wed girl led me to a neighboring room, where she introduced me to a deeply tanned, sturdy man, who appeared to be at the very least in his late thirties. I later found out he was her husband. We greeted each other with a polite nod. Then I climbed into Mureed's car, which at this point no longer reminded me of a shared taxi, and we drove off towards the coast.

The remaining leg of our journey was a hundred times more scenic than what I had seen earlier that day. I watched rugged white mountains gradually emerge from the dry plains, reflecting the golden evening sun like mirrors and guiding our car along smooth slopes until they finally exposed the sparkling sea.

Tall buildings eventually began to emerge from beyond the mountains and a well-paved road guided us along neatly planted greenery and flowerbeds until we were welcomed by a giant Iranian flag and colorful letters reading: I love Chabahar.

Chabahar is Iran's southernmost city, and its name roughly translates to Four Springs, since the weather remains roughly similar throughout the year. The city is located in a free-trade zone due to the importance of its harbor, which was constructed half a century ago under the Iranian Shah. Like Gwadar, Chabahar is an important access point to the Arabian Sea with plenty of foreign trade. However, I came to feel the two cities were worlds apart as soon as we entered Chabahar. From the tall structures and orderly traffic, to the neat ornamentation and lack of livestock roaming the streets, as well as the city's sheer size, Chabahar truly was decades ahead of Gwadar. Watching the city from outside of the car, I could not believe I was still in Balochistan.

A few kilometers outside of the metropolitan center, we arrived at Mureed's house. Like Dawood's village, Mureed's house was covered in beige clay and decorated with colorful *pashk* hanging in front of the building to dry. The only difference was that Mureed's home consisted of one single building and a separate bathroom with a water pump. There was no crowd of women outside to welcome me; instead, I was introduced to Mureed's wife, Gulrukh, and his two teenage daughters, who were inside the house.

Immediately, I noticed the strikingly similar physical traits among all members of the family. Like Mureed, Gulrukh and her two daughters all had deeply tanned skin, thick black hair, bright blue eyes, and a sturdy build. I had never in my life seen features like theirs, which made the women's soft smiles that accompanied their warm welcome hugs even more memorable to me. I joyfully returned their gestures and handed them a box of a buttery Pakistani sweet known as *sohan halwa*, which I had bought in Karachi.

However, as soon as I settled on the yellow-red carpet in a cool, air-conditioned room with Gulrukh and her daughters, a troublesome reality unfolded itself. With Mureed and Dawood disappeared to another room, there were no more Urdu speakers around me, and I faced a massive language barrier.

"Farsi?" was the first word out of the younger daughter's mouth after greeting me.

I shook my head.

"Balochi?" she followed up.

I replied with "*kamo, kamo*," indicating that I knew a little bit.

In response to this, the girls went on to talk to me like a cascading waterfall of words, but to my dismay, I did not understand a single word. It was then that I realized that while the dialects of Balochi spoken on the Pakistani side were rich in English and Urdu words, those on the Iranian side contained significantly more Persian words. Likewise, simple English phrases that were understood by almost everyone in Pakistan were of no use in Iran.

Embarrassed, I indicated my lack of comprehension with hand gestures, which the women reciprocated. The first gesture the women indicated to me was to take off my *chadar*, which I did. Then, I saw a look of urgency develop in the women's eyes as they pointed to my phone's camera lens and said "no." I immediately understood. At this point, I had become very much accustomed to the fact that photographing women was a major taboo in most Baloch families. I gave the women a gentle smile, assuring them I had understood and would respect their wishes.

We spent the next hour drinking pure black tea and smoking *chillim* together. The room was filled with awkward silence as we all became exhausted by our cumbersome attempts at communication. I had no internet access since my Pakistani SIM card received no signal in Iran, and I had given up asking the women for a Wi-Fi password when I realized they did not understand the word "internet." Eventually, I stepped out of the room to ask Dawood to share his hotspot, which he readily agreed to do. As soon as I connected to the internet, my phone buzzed with dozens of notifications for missed WhatsApp calls and messages from Jalal, Sanaullah, and Mureed. I frantically opened their chats, figuring something terrible had happened, just to read the same message over and over again: "Please don't take any photos of the women!!!"

Soon after, Mureed appeared in the doorway, informing me he would take us shopping that evening. I excitedly got ready and wrapped my embroidered *chadar* around my head. Gulrukh, however, stopped me at the last minute. She took off my *chadar* and handed me one of hers, which, in contrast to my bright orange embroidered one with glitter and mirrors, was plain and black with simple dark polka dots. *How ugly*, I thought, despite politely wearing it.

Mureed, Dawood, Gulrukh, and I squeezed into the black Toyota while the two daughters stayed at home to prepare dinner. We pulled out of the small settlement and drove along the well-paved coastal road until we entered the metropolitan area. Like a child in an amusement park, I watched the city lights from my window in amazement. *Feels like Karachi*, I thought to myself.

At one point, the lights intensified and eventually transformed into a huge complex of colorfully lit malls and food courts resembling the casinos of Las Vegas, followed by a large sign reading: CFZ – Chabahar Free Zone.

Mureed pulled up next to an ice cream shop in front of one of the many malls, where the four of us exited the car and sat down. It was already nine o'clock and I felt tired but overwhelmed. The bright lights surrounding me dazzled me even more than the excessive sweetness of the saffron ice cream I was slurping. Chabahar Free Zone was by all means a sensory overload for someone who had spent the previous night in a place like Surbandar.

"You and Dawood can go explore the malls. I will stay behind with my wife since she can't walk much," Mureed announced.

Without hesitation, Dawood and I entered the first mall, where the cold blows of the air-conditioning nearly froze the sweat on my skin into ice crystals. We immediately found ourselves surrounded by hundreds of East Asian electronic shops selling everything from cell phones to cameras, with occasional clothing, cosmetics, hardware, and even tire shops sprinkled in between. Every single item sold in this mall, from candy bars to fertilizer, was imported from abroad, seemingly at a discounted price like in a duty-free store. We strolled along all three floors of this mall, and then moved on to the next one, and the one after that. All malls followed the same design and offered the same random assortment of cheap imported goods. If anything, this shopping center reminded me of the endless electronics markets of Shenzhen in China. Not in my wildest dreams would I have expected to find such a place in Balochistan.

"Are you looking for something specific?" Dawood asked me after nearly two hours of directionless walking.

"I don't know," I mumbled.

It was only my first evening in Chabahar and all I was looking for was first impressions. Besides, I had not exchanged my money yet and had no Iranian tumans on me.

"Let's take a look at some clothing stores," I suggested out of curiosity.

Dawood led me to a floor full of clothing and textile stores. Their inventories resembled those of Chinese online shopping portals: thousands upon thousands of clothing pieces of questionable quality but unbeatable prices, accompanied by the pungent smells of synthetic dyes and materials. I incuriously scanned aisle after aisle, but nothing aroused my interest. Fair to say, I did not particularly regret not having any local currency on me.

"Where can I find *pashk*?" I eventually asked Dawood, who responded with utter surprise, "They don't have that in this mall. CFZ is mostly for imported goods. You must go to the local bazaar for this."

And so, our plan for the following day was born.

The next morning, Dawood and I left the house early to exchange my money and explore the market while avoiding the hottest hours of the day. Still, there were moments when I nearly fainted walking through the crowded lanes of Chabahar's traditional bazaar. Nearly overflowing with colorful textiles and shiny jewelry, and loud vendors selling herbs and spices in every corner, this place greatly resembled the traditional markets of Pakistan. I covered my face with the unappealing dark *chadar* that Gulrukh had lent me while admiring the many beautiful unstitched *doochi* fabrics hanging from the storefronts. I still could not comprehend why she made me wear dark fabric—which absorbed the heat—when I had so many nice, colorful *chadars* on me.

Strolling through the narrow lanes, I noticed many shops selling small stone blocks. Upon closer investigation, I noticed intricate patterns carved into the stones resembling those of *dooch*.

"These are stamps used to print designs onto fabric. They are the outline for embroidery," Dawood explained to me. This was perhaps the only thing he could tell me about women's clothing.

"I would like to buy a dress or two for myself. Machine-made, if possible," I said.

We continued to fight our way through the crowded market while the many sales pitches around us were deafening. Occasionally, we would pass women sitting on the floor selling a variety of unstitched, embroidered fabrics.

"Can you ask her for the price of the brown set?" I asked Dawood, who replied with a price in tumans.

I knew the exchange rate I had memorized from Google was not at all accurate, so instead of running long calculations in my head, I simply asked Dawood if this was a reasonable price.

He replied, "I don't know, this is the price the lady mentioned."

The look I returned to him summarized my reaction: *You didn't even try to haggle! What are you doing?* But, instead of speaking up, I chose to remain silent and scrap the idea of buying dresses altogether.

"I think I'm short on cash. I will buy my clothes when I return to Karachi. Let's go to the mobile shop so I can purchase an Iranian SIM card," I told Dawood.

Unfortunately, this plan was no more successful than our previous one since it was a public holiday, and all mobile shops were closed. *Oh well, I will survive one more day without internet*, I thought to myself.

Before I knew it, I was back at Mureed's home with Gulrukh and her daughters. As soon as I entered the premises, I was greeted by the smell of fresh seafood and spiced rice from the kitchen and grilled meat over burned wood from the outdoor fireplace. That was when I realized that the women had prepared a heavenly lunch consisting of fish biryani and my favorite, mutton sajji! Immediately, my stomach began to grumble and I could not wait for the women to spread out the plastic cloth on the floor and serve the delicacies. I dug into the food and quickly fell in love with all its sensations. I loved to feel the fish skin crack between my molars, mutton fat melt on my tongue, and biryani masala tingle every nerve in my mouth. This meal took me to seventh heaven, and I could not think of any place I would have rather been in that moment than Gulrukh's little ladies' chamber.

However, as soon as we had finished our meal and the two daughters ran off into the kitchen to do the dishes, the awkward feeling of the previous evening returned. Gulrukh and I sat across from each other in silence for the next fifteen minutes. We repeatedly exchanged awkward smiles. Endless combinations of English, Urdu, German, and even Chinese words were racing through my head, yet my tongue was paralyzed. No matter how badly I wanted to, I could not even try to speak because the fear of embarrassment and humiliation had become like a physical barrier for me. Although we could not exchange our thoughts in spoken language, the look in Gulrukh's dark-circled blue eyes was sufficient to suggest she must have felt the same.

Trying to distract myself from this strange situation, I resorted to my phone and opened WhatsApp, only to realize that Dawood's hotspot had disappeared. He must have left the house, and so had Mureed. I waited for the girls to return to the room, then I showed them the Wi-Fi symbol on my phone and complained. Both scrutinized the screen for a moment until I noticed a flash on their faces, and they suddenly exclaimed, "Ah, net!"

One of the first phrases I learned from Gulrukh and her daughters was "*Net aste?*" I used this phrase to ask if internet was available, which revealed itself to be synonymous with whether a man was in the house. I quickly realized that Gulrukh and her daughters possessed only simple button phones for calls, without internet access. Mureed and Dawood, in contrast, each owned smartphones, but since they were often outside of the house, I was left without internet access for most of the time. I typed out short messages explaining my situation and as soon as one of the men returned home, I would send them to Jalal, Sanaullah, and any family or friends who might worry about me.

Unable to converse, roam outside of the room, or connect to the World Wide Web, there was little to do other than watch the women go about their everyday tasks. Over time, I learned that, apart from household chores and the daily five prayers that are obligatory for Muslims, there was one task the women spent most of the day on: embroidery. From right after cleaning the dishes of one meal until beginning the preparation for the next, all three women would resort to their sewing kits and spend hour after hour weaving colorful threads along the dark pattern printed onto the fabric with stamps like the ones I had seen in the bazaar.

Noticing my careful attention to the women's work, one of the daughters eventually handed me her fabric and encouraged me to give it a try. I felt ecstatic as I saw in it an immersive cultural experience, a traveler's dream come true. I excitedly picked up thread and needle and followed the girl's instructions on where and how to puncture the fabric and pull the thread through. After finishing the first triangular design, I proudly admired the beautiful traditional shape I had just embroidered with my own hand. I smiled, and for a brief moment, I thought to myself: *Now I am just like a Baloch banuk!*

However, as I moved on and continued the work on similar designs, I soon realized what a dreadfully repetitive task embroidery truly was. I added stitch after stitch, as close to the previous one as possible, and with designs as elaborate as *dooch*, the task felt endless—seemingly an ideal activity for situations like the one I was in. After embroidering a few more shapes, I handed the fabric back to the girl. I now understood why it took months to finish a *pashk*, even for women who dedicated every waking hour to it.

Not long after, the doorbell rang, and within seconds, there were about a dozen new pairs of sparkling blue eyes in our little room. Some aunts and their children from the village had come over for a visit. We exchanged hugs and kisses as a greeting and the aunts began speaking to me in Balochi. I tried my best to respond using the words and phrases I had picked up that afternoon. Meanwhile, Gulrukh left the room to prepare *chillim* and passed it around to the guests, while her daughters rushed into the kitchen to prepare tea.

After a few rounds of *chai* and *chillim*, boredom once again set in. While the women and children around me entertained each other by gossiping and laughing out loud, I was left alone in the corner staring holes into the blank walls of the room. I opened the Facebook app on my phone to mindlessly scroll through my unrefreshed feed from three days ago and read the same few posts over and over again. I had downloaded multiple encryption apps prior to my trip to access social media platforms that are censored in Iran, but without internet connection for the majority of the time, I had not had the chance to test them out. *This is worse than the wedding in Lasbela*, I thought.

Suddenly, an idea came to my mind. With a dozen visitors from out of town, at least one of them must have access to the internet, right? With a bright smile full of hope, I interrupted the women's gossip and asked the round, "*Net aste*?"

In response, murmurs erupted as the women looked around and pulled small button phones out of their *pendols*.

Most of them only had simple call and text features and contact lists with a handful of saved numbers, but no access to internet, let alone mobile hotspot. Suddenly, however, one woman spoke up. She had come with her son in tow, who appeared to be aged around ten. The woman called her son over, who handed her his smartphone with internet access. With glee in my eyes, I connected to the boy's hotspot. I knew this would only be a temporary solution, because the boy would soon run off again with his phone. Still, I was overjoyed to have at least *something*. I used my five minutes of internet access to send a message to Jalal: *Hi, I hope you are doing fine. I am well and safe here with Mureed's family. However, I still don't have internet access in this house, and the language barrier is huge. It's very hard to communicate my needs to the family, and I get bored easily. Please, let me know if you can think of any solution to this problem.*

I pressed "send" right on time, before the boy, and with him the internet connection, disappeared. Relieved to have at least sent a message and refreshed my Facebook feed, I redirected my attention to the women's laughter. They were still passing around the *chillim* and inhaling deep puffs one after another. *Perhaps becoming addicted to nicotine helps with boredom*, I thought to myself.

Like the previous night, dinner was served late, around midnight. We had deep-fried fish with spicy sauce, not the lightest food to eat in the middle of the night. As soon as everyone had finished eating and the floor was cleaned up, Gulrukh and her daughters pulled out a couple of blankets and rolled them out on the carpet. The guests did not leave but selected spots on the cushioned floor, turned off the light, and went to sleep.

Soon, I was surrounded by loud snores from all directions. Sharing a room with large numbers of strangers barely bothered me, as I had done this many times in Pakistan. Rather, it was indigestion that prevented me from falling asleep immediately after dinner. I tried to sit upright to avoid heartburn from the oily food, but there was little space. My phone was charging across the room and did not want to wake the others up; hence, I spent the next two hours sitting silently in the darkness, with occasional trips to the toilet outside the house. After all, I had to release all the tea I had consumed with my meal.

When I felt like most of the grease had finally moved on to my intestines, I quietly spread out my limbs, careful not to wake anyone up, closed my eyes, and tried to sleep. *Finally, this day has come to an end*, I thought. Soon after I had dozed off, however, I was torn out of my dreams by a shriek: "*Amma!*" One of the children in the room had begun to panic, and as the mother tried to console her crying daughter, I let out a quiet sigh. This atrocious cycle would only repeat itself for the rest of the night.

Plagued by headaches from a sleepless night, I woke up when the women around me arose for *fajr*, the early morning prayer right before sunrise. I tried to fall back asleep but was soon greeted with a typical Iranian breakfast consisting of flatbread, cream spread, butter, jelly, and of course, unlimited black tea. Instead of rest, I chose the latter to get me through the day. I drank cup after cup until I had downed a good liter of tea—kind of like the women could not stop smoking *chillim* all day.

Sometime after breakfast, I briefly got a hold of Dawood and connected to his mobile hotspot. Alongside the many notifications for meme pages and funny videos that buzzed through my phone, there was also a new message from Jalal, which read: *Hi Bela, I'm sorry to hear about that. I just called up all my contacts in Chabahar and one of them found a relative who speaks English who is willing to host you. He said he will pick you up this afternoon.*

I nearly jumped in circles for joy. Jalal had found me another host! That afternoon, I would move into another home, where I could hopefully hold conversations and properly get to know the family.

I went into the adjacent room, where Gulrukh's elder daughter approached me with a stack of fresh laundry. She pointed towards the pile, mimicked a washing motion with her hands, and said, "*Man shosht.*"

I understood that she had washed my dirty clothes and added the new phrase to my mental dictionary. Overall, I was surprised at how much Balochi I had picked up during my short stay with Mureed's family. I had always had difficulties learning languages outside of traditional classroom settings and used to think it was impossible to study a new language without heavy textbooks and strict teachers. For Balochi, however, there are no textbooks available in bookstores, and colleges do not offer introductory language courses. The language is not listed in any language learning apps; it is mostly passed on at home from parent to child. I had never imagined spending much thought on a language like Balochi but the unexpected situation at Mureed's home left me without a choice. It felt like I had been thrown into the sea and was forced to paddle to stay afloat. Well, not that I was complaining—learning a new language is always a worthwhile investment.

I picked up my clean clothes and squeezed them into my suitcase—not an easy task with so much *dooch*! Mureed's family seemed to have been informed about my plans and helped me pack my belongings. I returned the ugly dark *chadar* to Gulrukh and left out a red *doochi* one to wear later. In the meantime, the guests from the previous day had already left and new guests trickled in. There rarely seemed to be a day without guests in the house.

Sometime in the afternoon, Mureed knocked on the door and informed me he would take me to meet my new host. I wrapped my red *chadar* around my head and exchanged goodbyes with his daughters. I followed Mureed and Gulrukh into the car and squeezed myself onto the seat. On the way, Mureed dropped Gulrukh off at a tailor shop, where she dropped off a stack of pre-printed fabrics to have them machine embroidered, a time-saving alternative to the traditional hand embroidery. Then, he drove towards the main city beach, where I would meet my new host.

Throughout the drive, conflicting emotions were racing through my head. On the one hand, I felt sad to leave Gulrukh and her lovely daughters. Despite the language barrier, I could feel the benevolence and care for their guests in their eyes, and looking back, I felt grateful for every minute I got to spend with them, no matter how bored I may have been. On the other hand, however, the complexity of the situation had resulted in pent-up frustration that I had never experienced before. For perhaps the first time in my travel history, a host family treated me as a guest, a family friend, rather than a tourist from overseas. They did not use online platforms to meet travelers from the other end of the world, and they did not charge money as a guesthouse would. Rather, they welcomed me alongside their family members and offered me the same entertainment as all other female guests, which I jokingly referred to as "*chai*, *chillim*, and chill." In short, they treated me just like a Baloch *banuk*—although I thought I was just like a man?

"Nice to meet you and welcome to Chabahar!" a man in his late twenties welcomed me in excellent English. "My name is Moslem and I heard about you from a friend of a friend of a friend."

The young man transferred my luggage to the trunk of his car, which was parked near the beach promenade. "Have you had the chance to explore the area yet?" he asked me, to which I shook my head.

"Let's have a stroll along the beach then!" he suggested.

I followed Moslem's steps down to the beach, surprised at how he managed to keep his carefully ironed white *shalwar kameez* clean while making his way through the moist sand. His tall and slim stature cast an elongated shade in it, while his lightly tanned skin reflected the golden afternoon sun. Moslem's hair and eyes were the same shade of medium brown, and unlike most Baloch men, he had neither a beard nor a mustache. His neatly put-together appearance reflected that of a businessman, and my assumption was not false.

"I'm an independent businessman focusing on import and export of hardware here in Chabahar," he told me while walking.

"I also used to live in China for a while to facilitate trade from there," he added.

Excited to have met a fellow foreigner who had lived in China, I playfully tested his language skills by asking, "*Ni hui shuo zhongwen ma*?" ("Do you speak Chinese?").

To my amazement, he replied in perfectly fluent Mandarin, and went on to talk about his experience in the country. He claimed to have learned the language by immersion only, and within the timespan of just one year, which made his knowledge even more impressive.

"I also learned a bit of Balochi while living with my previous hosts," I bragged.

However, when I tried to hold a simple communication in his native language, Moslem had trouble understanding.

"I think your previous hosts spoke a Makrani dialect," he eventually interrupted me.

"Our family is from Taftan, far inland, and our dialect is completely different."

After a few minutes of walking, we reached the busy part of the beach, which was crowded with families, animals, and street vendors, just like Seaview Beach in Karachi. There were plenty of camel owners who offered rides on their animals for a small fee.

"Do you want to give it a try?" Moslem asked.

Without hesitation, I agreed. I had ridden camels many times before but getting up close to these majestic creatures was always a delight.

I excitedly mounted the camel, holding tightly onto my red *chadar* to prevent it from being blown off by the strong breeze. Moslem handed a few bills to the camel owner, who then walked us along a short stretch of the beach and back. While I enjoyed great views of the crowded beach from the back of the tall animal, I saw Moslem's expression grow slightly concerned as he followed along. He alternated turning his head towards the crowds and then back to me.

Eventually, after I dismounted the camel, he awkwardly asked me, "Don't you have another *chadar* with you?"

"What do you mean?" I replied, confused.

"I have a couple of different *doochi chadars* and *dupattas* in my suitcase," I added.

"No, no . . ." Moslem dismissed my response.

"Don't you have any black *chadar* with you?"

My clueless expression was likely sufficient to suggest that I did not.

"Look around, all the women here wear black *chadars*," he pointed out.

"You're the only one wearing a colorful *chadar*, that's why people are staring at you."

I was taken aback for a moment. What was wrong about my *doochi chadar* that Gulrukh had lent me her dark *chadar* and now Moslem also voiced his concern?

"Is there a law against colorful *chadars* here?" I asked.

"No, no, it's not against the law," Moslem explained. "It's just that if you wear a Balochi dress, you *must* wear a black *chadar* with it."

"But I bought this dress as a three-piece suit. This *chadar* came with it and I've never had a problem wearing it. In fact, almost everyone wears colorful *chadars* in Pakistan," I argued.

"Maybe in Pakistan it's different. They like everything colorful," Moslem mumbled.

"But here, Baloch girls only wear black *chadars* in public, and it looks very bad if you wear this colorful *chàdar* in combination with *pashk*."

Noticing the disappointment on my face, he assured me, "No worries, when we get home my wife will lend you her black *chadar*."

Moslem and I spent some more time strolling along the *Darya Bozorg*, or Big Sea, as this beach is locally known, to admire the large waves from afar since entering the water in this spot was too dangerous. We also climbed up green algae-covered cliffs where mysterious blowholes unexpectedly erupted and splashed water directly into my face. Moslem seemed to have great fun capturing my funny expressions when the water hit me with his phone camera. I, however, had become hyper-focused on the people around me. Were they actually staring at me or was it all in my head? Is it all my *chadar*'s fault? Are colorful *chadars* really that bad? For a moment, I felt as if I was back in Lasbela, trying to enjoy myself at a wedding while unknowingly harming the reputation of my host family by attracting the stares and gossips of the crowd.

Later that evening, we arrived at Moslem's home in the neighboring village of Tis. Unlike Chabahar, which is a development of the twentieth century, Tis is an ancient fishing village dating back to the times of Alexander the Great. Instead of bustling shopping malls like the CFZ, this quiet small town offers a variety of historical sites, including mysterious caves from ancient times, ruins of a fort left behind by the Portuguese, and even a cemetery for *jinns*! With its peaceful gardens and calm family friendly beaches, Tis carried a significantly more laid-back vibe.

Moslem ushered me into his house, which was similar but larger and more polished than the homes I had previously visited. We were swiftly welcomed by a girl and three boys, who gestured to us to sit down on the carpet, where a can of black tea and fresh fruits were waiting for us.

"Welcome to my home! This is my wife, Maryam, and these boys are my nephews," Moslem introduced me to his family.

Without saying a word, Maryam extended her pale, skinny hand from underneath her black *chadar*, which she wore even at home. I briefly glanced at her face; she had very fair, youthful skin, and timid dark-brown eyes that immediately broke contact with me when I looked at her.

"Try to guess my wife's age," Moslem urged me after I had correctly estimated his age to be twenty-six.

I took another look at the girl. Her features appeared very youthful and resembled those of a teenager but considering that she was married to a man in his mid-twenties, I assumed my perception must be false.

"Twenty-two?" I guessed.

Moslem tried to hold his laughter. He translated my estimate to Maryam, who also began to chuckle.

"She's seventeen!" Moslem revealed.

I was in shock. No wonder Moslem's wife appeared younger than me as in fact she was four years my junior.

"That's so young!" I exclaimed.

"It is how it is," Moslem mumbled.

"We only got married three months ago. She's currently pregnant with our first child."

I looked at the girl's frail body. It was hard to imagine that under her wide black *chadar* a small bump might be hiding.

"That must be so painful! The first weeks of pregnancy are the most difficult," I cluelessly regurgitated what I had read in my ninth-grade biology textbook.

Maryam shyly smiled at me. It quickly became apparent that her husband was the only one in the family who understood English.

"Well, I hope she gets all the rest she needs," I added.

To my dismay, however, the girl had already disappeared into the kitchen to continue the dinner preparations.

Right before dinner was ready, a group of four women arrived: one middle-aged lady, one who appeared to be in her late-twenties, and two girls with an infant and a toddler in tow.

"This is my second mother, my sister, and these two are my cousins, who are also married to my brothers," Moslem introduced the women.

"Oh, and the girls are also my wife's sisters," he added.

I replied with a confused look, to which Moslem explained, "My second mother is my father's second wife. She is not my mother, but she is like a mother to me. My sister is her daughter, but not my mother's daughter. From the same father, we are fifteen siblings: eight children from my first mother and seven children from my second mother. We all marry our cousins from the same side of the family, so all my brothers are married to my wife's sisters."

My brain was overwhelmed by this influx of confusing information, so instead of wasting my mental capacity on drawing a huge family tree in my head, I shifted my attention to the adorable baby in one of the girls' arms.

"How old is this sweetheart?" I asked.

"She's only three months old," Moslem's sister replied in fluent English.

"This is Zainab's second child," the woman gestured towards one of the girls, who appeared to be an elder clone of Moslem's wife.

"Her first child is two years old," she pointed at the toddler.

Having picked up my obsession with people's ages, Moslem added, "Zainab herself is twenty-one right now, just like you, and already has two children."

He gestured towards the other girl and said, "Sana is sixteen years old and five months pregnant."

Suddenly, Zainab extended her hands holding her little baby daughter to me and smiled.

"She's offering you to hold her daughter," Moslem's sister explained.

Excited and honored to have won the young mother's trust, I accepted the bundle of cuteness and gently placed her on my lap. *Three-month-olds are so heavy*, was my first thought. However, I quickly became so enamored with the baby's bulging black eyes, soft skin, and irresistibly adorable smile that I forgot about the growing weight in my arms and everything else around me. Zainab passed me a bottle of milk and instructed me to feed to the baby. Soon enough, I found myself holding and feeding the cutest little human being I had ever seen and noticed an overflow of feel-good hormones thrashing through my brain. *How amazing it must be to have children of one's own*, I imagined. *I wish I could be like these girls and get married young*, I thought for a brief second, painfully oblivious to all the hardships and responsibilities that come with marriage and motherhood. *What does it feel like to be pregnant and give birth, raise children and run a household?* Endless questions went through my head. All I knew was that at least for a good couple of years, I would not know the answers. According to the society I grew up in, all I should worry about at age twenty-one was studying hard, getting into a good grad school, and landing a well-paying job.

As I was holding the baby in my arms, Moslem's sister started a conversation with me. Her name was Zahra and she worked as an English teacher at a local school. She was two years older than Moslem and had two sons.

"Most women here have eight, nine, ten children, but for me, two are enough," she told me.

"My sons are the only people in our family with Persian names. My father was very angry about this, so he gave them alternative Arabic names. Until today, he only addresses them with their Arabic names because he thinks it's more Islamic."

Zahra was very interested in my travel stories from around the world. She listened attentively when I told her about my plans for traveling in Iran.

In the end, she said, "You're very lucky you get to explore Iran. For years, I've been dreaming of visiting Shiraz, but money is tight. We simply can't afford to travel to other cities. The economic situation in Iran is very bad."

Zahra seemed very educated and open-minded, and I enjoyed talking to her. Later on, I realized she was the only woman in Chabahar who I talked to directly and openly, without the help of a man as a translator. We exchanged our numbers and promised to stay in touch with each other.

After the women left, Moslem's wife served the dinner she had been preparing. As in all the previous homes I had visited, we also gathered on the floor, and Moslem's wife spread out a plastic cloth on top of which she placed the food. The meal consisted of plain white rice and a piece of boiled bony meat, served alongside a large glass of milk and lots of *naan.* Not having eaten anything since I left Mureed's house in the afternoon, I hungrily dug in. However, the meal lacked much flavor, by which I mean spices. Overall, it reminded me of all the plain boiled food I ate during my time in Kurdistan. I cannot remember how much weight I lost on that trip, but it was a lot.

Moslem, who must have noticed the disappointment on my face, asked, "How do you like my wife's cooking?"

Trying to be polite, I replied, "It's pretty good, it's just that I'm used to eating very spicy food."

"Yes, most people here in Chabahar also eat very spicy. They're just like Pakistanis. But our family is from Taftan, near Zahedan, and we don't eat as much spicy food there," Moslem replied.

"By the way, these tomatoes are homegrown from our village. You should give them a try!" He pointed at a plate of salad with freshly sliced tomatoes.

I savored a slice and immediately fell in love with its meaty, juicy, tangy flavor. This was by far the most delicious tomato I had ever eaten, even beating the ones I had in rural Montenegro as a teen. I quickly abandoned the rice and the bony meat and devoured slice after slice of this incredible fruit. Needless to say, the Taftani tomatoes became a staple of my diet during my stay with Moslem's family, alongside the fresh apricots from their village, which were just as delicious.

Over the next few days, Moslem tried his best to show me around the area, despite his busy schedule as a businessman. He took me climbing to the mysterious ancient caves and the

Portuguese castle of Tis, and we went snorkeling in the warm, shallow water of Darya Kuchek, which translates to "small sea." One day, we went on a day trip eastward along the coast, covering Makran's most scenic natural sites like the pink saline lake, the uniquely shaped Martian Mountains, and the stunning tall white cliffs of Beris—places so beautiful that I frequently exchanged the plain black *chadar* that Maryam had given me with a colorful *doochi dupatta* for the photos' sake. On these trips, Moslem usually brought along his three nephews, who were aged between eight and fourteen, while his wife stayed home and focused on the household chores. Hence, every evening I was guaranteed to return to an impeccably clean room and neatly arranged luggage, fresh laundry, and warm food.

On the surface, everything seemed perfect. Behind closed doors however, I often overheard arguments between Moslem and Maryam. She seemed overwhelmed and I could see the tiredness in her eyes every time her husband told her to cook or do the laundry. I could hardly imagine the stress of being newly married, pregnant, and in charge of so many tasks at such a young age. I felt bad about myself for being an additional mouth to feed, plate to clean, dress to wash, and room to tidy. Hospitality is an important aspect of Balochi culture, and families go above and beyond to make their guests feel welcome. Unfortunately, their sacrifices are not always obvious to the untrained eye, and unaware of the cultural context, travelers rarely overstay their welcome.

One evening, I received a text message from Moslem while he was out of the house: *"Hey Arabela, I hope everything is OK. Starting from tomorrow, work will be very busy for me, and I will be unable to spend time with you. I can help you find bus tickets to another city if you want."*

I took this as a sign that it was time to leave. I realized I had already stayed in Chabahar for a week at this point, leaving me with only two more weeks on my twenty-day Iran visa! How was I supposed to visit all those amazing palaces and gardens in western Iran that had motivated me to embark on this journey in the first place in such a short time? Not wanting to be a burden for Moslem's family, I agreed to start looking for bus tickets out of Chabahar. My plan was to visit Bandar Abbas next. Unfortunately, neither Moslem nor I was able to find any bus route to Bandar Abbas, and even the buses to Shiraz were booked out days in advance. Eventually, I decided to stay in Tis for a few more days until transportation became available while trying to be as little of a burden as possible for Moslem's family.

The next couple of days were no different from my time at Mureed's home: Endless long afternoons sitting in a room and drinking tea, unable to communicate with anyone due to the language barrier and trying to distract my mind by picking up embroidery. The only difference was that I had a SIM card by this point, and I could at least scroll through my social media feeds. I stayed in contact with various acquaintances in Iran, all of whom promised to help get my hands on a bus ticket, but none of them was successful. It also did not help that my period kicked in during those days, and when I asked for painkillers, I was met with the response: "We are a Muslim family; we don't do drugs."

Eventually, I came up with an idea to keep myself busy without causing trouble to Moslem's family. I could just go out and explore by myself, like I normally do when I travel! Of course, I was aware that I was still in Balochistan, where women rarely step outside of the house alone, but what could be the worst that would happen if I went for a stroll by myself in this sleepy village? It seemed to be worth a try at least. I informed

Moslem about my plan, expecting him to simply show me where the doorbell was so I could return by myself. But he told me to wait for his eight-year-old nephew Yousuf to accompany me. Going outside alone seemed to be off the table for me, just like for a Baloch *banuk*.

Yousuf took me for a walk through the village. It was close to *maghrib*, the time for early evening prayer, which meant that the streets were even quieter than usual. There were a few boys playing in the streets and groups of women walking from house to house, covering their faces with their black *chadars* as soon as they spotted us. Yousuf led me off the main streets across sand dunes and thorn bushes, hardly noticing my struggles as a woman in long clothes that always got entangled. We climbed up a small hill overlooking the nearby settlements until we reached a graveyard.

"*Insan*!" the boy said while pointing at the simple stone tombs around us, indicating that humans were buried there. He made a stepping motion with his feet and said "no!" I understood that we were not allowed to step on the tombs.

We moved onto tombs that resembled the previous ones but were flatter and contained mysterious carvings. To my horror, Moslem's nephew walked right across the tombs, stepping on the stones. Before I could voice my shock, he pointed at the carvings and exclaimed, "*Jinn*!"

I realized he had taken me to the Qabrestan-e-Jinn, a cemetery where, alongside humans, invisible ghost-like creatures named *jinn* allegedly lay buried. I was unable to find out much information about the origins of this spooky place, but it certainly seemed to be a breeding ground of creativity for eight-year-olds like Moslem's nephew.

Afterwards, we toured the village further, admiring the simple yet beautiful ancient white mosques, which provided a magical contrast to the lavender-colored evening sky. Not much later, the melodic call for prayer loudly sounded from their minarets, marking the end of yet another uneventful day in Balochistan. I had gotten used to spending long days at home at this point and accepted it as an integral part of traveling in Balochistan as a woman. Just because Jalal thought I was "just like a man" did not mean that everyone else would treat me as such. I covered my face with my black *chadar* as a group of men passed by me on their way to the mosque. They did not glance at me and neither did anyone else we had run into in this village. I wondered if they all accepted me as a local or if they knew I was a guest from foreign lands.

One fact I knew for certain, however, was that with every passing day in Balochistan, I embraced the local culture more and more, be it in the way I dressed, acted, and even thought. I no longer felt like just a foreign tourist who traveled and observed, immune to all the unwritten social rules that applied to locals. I now accepted that I would just go with the flow and immerse myself in the surroundings. Over time, I gave up trying to fight the restrictions that came with being a woman in Balochistan and began appreciating them as an integral part of my travel experience. I was a woman, and I was being treated very differently to the way I was back at home, but nonetheless, I felt respected. Day by day I was becoming just like a Baloch *banuk* and no longer minded it.

CHAPTER FIVE

GOOD GIRL, BAD GIRL

It soon became dark, and following his uncle's advice, Yousuf decided to cover the relatively short distance home by taxi.

We got into a dusty black car, where we were greeted by a young, well-groomed man in dress shirt and pants. He asked for directions to our place, which Moslem's nephew provided. The two then struck up a conversation and, eventually, the boy revealed that I was a foreigner.

Excitedly, the driver turned towards me and introduced himself in fluent English. "Hi, my name is Mohamed and I work as an engineer. I'm thirty-three years old, married, with two children. I drive taxi in my free time to supplement my income and support my family."

I politely returned the pleasantries and introduced myself. Then, our conversation took off. We talked about our lifestyles, interests, travels, and anything else that might interest someone during a first encounter. I was impressed by Mohamed's English skills and interest in foreign cultures, and it was admirable to hear how hard he worked to provide for his family, spending all day away from his wife and children. Overall, we had a short but pleasant chat and Mohamed seemed to be a wholesome person.

Nonetheless, there was something that struck me wrong about Mohamed throughout our short chat. Perhaps it was the fact that he smiled too much, or maybe he was a little too enthusiastic about talking to me. I wasn't sure but I brushed off my doubts. Mohamed was just a friendly young Baloch who was excited to finally meet a foreigner in his village.

When we reached home, Mohamed handed me a small piece of paper with his phone number scribbled on it and said, "If you ever need a taxi to travel anywhere around Chabahar, please call this number. I promise, I will offer you the lowest fares."

I took the piece of paper and put it in my *pendol*. Mohamed and I exchanged goodbyes, and I followed Moslem's nephew inside the house, where dinner was waiting for us.

Throughout the evening, I kept thinking about Mohamed's offer. There were no buses available out of Chabahar until the weekend, and I did not want to bother Moslem's family unnecessarily. There was one last spot in Balochistan that I was dying to visit before moving on to the rest of Iran. The place in question was a peaceful, remote beach about two hours west of Chabahar called Darak. According to locals, the smooth golden-sand desert in this spot extends all the way into the sea, with a single date palm tree standing strong in front of the clashing waves. It was far away, but undoubtedly somewhere I would enjoy, I thought.

After counting my remaining cash for the next two weeks, I decided to call Mohamed and propose the route to him. He checked the fares of his competitors and then called me back with an offer to take me to Darak Beach and a nearby mud volcano for one hundred thousand tumans—less than thirty US dollars at the time. I consulted with Moslem, who agreed this fare was a steal for such a long drive, so I called back Mohamed and confirmed my plans for the next morning.

Excited for the upcoming day trip, I still could not shake off the uncomfortable feeling I had during my conversation with Mohamed. He was courteous in front of Moslem's nephew, but would he be the same when I was alone with him for a whole day? How would a regular man think of a woman who travels alone in a place like Balochistan? How would my willingness to hire a private driver be interpreted by a local? Up until this point,

I had had exclusively positive experiences with Baloch men, and I recalled what I'd been told: *"Having a woman with you in Balochistan is like traveling with a hundred weapons. Nobody will dare to harm you if you are with a woman. That's how much Baloch men respect women."*

On the other hand, I also recalled the worry on Jalal's face when he sent me off to Chabahar by myself. This insight may be correct for the majority of cases, but what about the minority where it is not? *Probably I'm just overreacting*, I thought to myself, although experience had taught me that a woman's sixth sense is rarely off.

To soothe my mind, I asked Moslem if one of his nephews could accompany me the next day, but he said everyone was busy with school. I called up my other acquaintances from Chabahar, but nobody was available at such short notice. Hence, I decided to take the chance and travel alone with Mohamed. After all, I was certain I would regret missing out on Darak Beach if I decided otherwise. Little did I know I would soon get to see an entirely different face of Balochistan.

The next morning, I woke up to ten missed calls. Mohamed had been waiting for me since the early morning hours. Now it was starting to get late and there was no time to waste so I quickly got dressed. I decided to wear the same orange *pashk* I had worn on my way to Gwadar, with the thin *dupatta* that came with the suit wrapped tightly around my head and fastened with a brooch underneath the black *chadar*. I applied light makeup and put on a plain surgical mask for modesty. Then, I stepped out of the door, where Mohamed was waiting for me in his dusty black car.

I immediately noticed the strong scent of musk emanating from Mohamed's neatly ironed dress shirt. His light-brown hair was sleekly combed back with an excess of gel, and the stubbles on his chin indicated his beard was freshly shaved. He was wearing sparkly sunglasses and a fake Rolex watch, dressed for a fine night out rather than a trip to the beach.

"Come on, sit in the front," he urged me as I opened the back door of the car. Mohamed presented a two-liter thermos of black tea and a bag containing hot *naan*, nuts, and dates. "I got you some breakfast. Besides, the view is much better in the front."

Usually, a driver asking a female passenger to sit in the front is a huge red flag, but the steaming hot tea and sweet Bam dates smelled too tempting for my empty stomach, so I reluctantly agreed and moved to the front seat.

Our journey began with innocent small talk as we quickly made our way out of the sleepy town, and I felt comfortable enough to lift my mask and *chadar*.

"Look, this is the traditional men's clothing here in Balochistan. It's very different from the clothes I'm wearing," Mohamed said, pointing towards some men on the road.

I faked my astonishment as if I had never seen *shalwar kameez* before.

Then he asked, "Which clothes do you prefer on men? Western-style or Balochi?"

Weirded out by this unusual question, I dryly replied, "Balochi."

"Oh no!!!" Mohamed cried out. "If I had known this, I would have worn traditional clothes today! But my wife says she likes Western clothes, so I thought you would too."

Oh God, this is going to be an interesting day, I thought to myself.

As soon as we got on the main road, the conversation took a more personal turn.

"Are you single?" Mohamed asked.

"I'm happily married," I lied.

"Oh . . ." I noticed Mohamed's expression change.

"But where's your husband?"

"He's in Chabahar for work right now." I made up a story. "We came here on a business trip, and I decided to travel around a bit during my free time."

"Ha, your husband must be so angry at me right now," Mohamed chuckled.

"Why would he be?" I asked.

"Because you're going out with another boy today," he grinned.

My stomach turned inside out when I realized my suspicions had been correct all along. But what could I do at this point? I was already in his car and out of town, and with mobile signal gradually disappearing, all I could do was bite my tongue and pull through this. After all, as a solo female traveler, I was very much used to situations like these.

Only a few minutes later, we found ourselves on an empty road, surrounded by nothing but desert, rocks, and camels—lots of camels.

"This road gets very dangerous at night. It's important that we make it back to Chabahar before sunset," Mohamed explained.

Unsettled by these remarks, I asked, "Dangerous in what way? Is it because of the road conditions, or robbers, or rebel groups?"

"No, no," Mohamed replied. "It's dangerous because of the camels."

I politely laughed at his seemingly pathetic attempt to crack a joke. *Why did this idiot have to scare me like that*, I thought.

"I'm serious, these camels are very dangerous at night," Mohamed said sternly, sweat dripping from his face.

I stuck my fingers outside of the window as we passed by a camel up close. How could these calm, non-stop-chewing peaceful creatures possibly be dangerous?

"See, they always block the road," Mohamed explained, pressing the brakes to let a camel cross the road in front of us. "In daylight it's easy to see them and drive carefully, but at night they're barely visible. Many bad accidents happen because of this, and my wife tells me every day to avoid this road after dark."

I nodded, despite still not understanding why camels were his biggest concern. *Oh well, not like I would want to be out after sunset with this guy, anyway*, I assured myself.

Throughout the drive, I kept my hand outside the window, despite it being broiled by the scorching midday sun. I still had hope of petting a camel or two this way as we drove by. *How lucky these animals are to just spend all day in this beautiful desert, doing nothing but grazing on shrubs and blocking the road.* I fantasized about being one of them. At least I would get to enjoy these gorgeous views in peace, without being interrupted by an annoying driver every five seconds.

Eventually, we turned onto a small dirt path that led to the tall mud volcano of Tang. There was an open gate and an unmanned ticket booth alongside a table listing entrance fees for various types of visitors: children, students, adults, and foreigners. Mohamed honked a few times, but nobody showed up, so we proceeded to enter the park without paying.

Mohamed parked his dusty black car on the brittle clay terrain in a spot where the cracks in the ground were not yet wide enough to swallow the vehicle's wheels. We stepped out and walked towards the tall mountain of mud emerging in front of us. I soon began to feel the ground bulging underneath the soles of my *sawas*, and not long after, we began the steep ascent towards the top of the volcano. Seeing me struggle in my grip-less footwear and heavy dress, Mohamed repeatedly offered his hand to me to hold onto. I declined every time, although I really could have used some help. Men way too often take advantage of such situations to touch a woman.

Completely out of breath, I eventually reached the top of the volcano while Mohamed was still climbing up, from where I admired stunning aerial views of the surrounding landscape. *I must film this*, I thought, and dashed forward with my open phone camera.

"Be careful, there is . . ." Mohamed yelled out, but it was too late.

He was interrupted by a loud SPLASH, and all of a sudden, I found half of my dy submerged in thick clay. My worst nightmare had come true: I had fallen into a volcano!

My first instinct was to kick my legs and push myself forward as if I were swimming, but to no avail, as I only found myself sinking deeper and deeper, being swallowed alive by the sticky grey substance. *That's it*, I thought: *My obituary will read: "Cause of death: drowned in a mud volcano."*

Fortunately, Mohamed was quick to act. He ran to the top at seemingly the speed of light and did what he was best at:

reaching out his hand. Unlike the previous times, I gladly grabbed onto it this time and let him pull me out with all his strength. *He must be so happy now*, I thought, rolling my eyes so hard they nearly bulged out of my skull.

After emerging from the muddy death trap, I burst out laughing. How *stupid* could I be to fall into a volcano! Deep inside, I knew the real reason why I ran so fast was in rebellion against a creepy driver, who was a little too eager to offer me his hand, but ironically, his dream came true because of this accident. Mohamed chuckled while helping me clean my hands, clothes, and the hundred thousand tumans that I had been keeping in my *pendol*. I wanted to slap his face with my *sawas* for touching a strange woman, but then I thought perhaps I should be a bit more grateful to the man who literally saved my life.

After the volcano incident, the mood between Mohamed and me became significantly more relaxed as both of us struggled to get over this mad event. All the frustration against this man that had been building up inside of me was temporarily relieved by his heroic actions. *Maybe Mohamed isn't that bad after all*, I thought. For some reason, women tend to forgive men way too easily. Somehow, one decent action from a man prompts a woman to ignore hundreds of red flags.

"Who are you texting all this time?" Mohamed interrupted me as we were leaving the park.

"My husband," I replied.

It was sort of true. I had been texting my boyfriend since entering the park, one of the few spots with mobile reception along this road.

"Didn't you say he was busy with work in Chabahar?" Mohamed asked. "If that is so, how come he has all this time on his hands to reply to your texts?"

That was when it hit me: *Oh crap, he has been monitoring me very closely all this time!*

I stuttered unintelligibly, trying to keep my white lie on life support.

"Tell me the truth," Mohamed said with a smirk. "You aren't actually traveling with your husband, are you?"

Being the helplessly honest person that I am, I admitted the truth: I was a solo female traveler, not yet married, and my partner was thousands of miles away from me.

"I knew it from the beginning!" Mohamed laughed. "But why did you lie to me? I'm a good guy! You can be honest about everything with me."

Needless to say, this short exchange quickly restored my level of frustration with Mohamed.

We continued our drive along the camel road, passing through a few villages here and there, until we reached a mountainous section of the road. Mohamed's sense of direction became less and less confident at this point, and he frequently had to stop and ask local shepherds for the way, all of whom pointed in different directions. His expression grew visibly more stressed as the late afternoon sun painted the surrounding rocks in warm golden hues. It was getting late, and we hadn't even reached Darak Beach yet. How could we possibly make it back to Tis before sunset?

We sighed with relief after one elderly shepherd finally pointed us in the right direction, and the golden rocks were gradually replaced by date palms and sand dunes. We were only a few kilometers away from the last destination on my Balochistan bucket list! Mohamed pressed the gas pedal since we were the only vehicle on this completely empty road. I stretched my hand out of the window to enjoy the increasingly salty breeze and could hardly believe my eyes as I admired the gorgeous landscape: a picturesque golden-sand desert with occasional palm trees and camels sprinkled in, sparkling turquoise waves emerging from the horizon, and a perfectly cloudless sky that was continuously changing into warmer tones of blue in preparation for sunset. It felt like a dream from *One Thousand and One Nights*, a fantasy version of the Middle East that only children could imagine.

Mohamed parked his car at the very beginning of the beach, where tall sand dunes made it difficult for regular cars to drive. I decided to leave behind my *burqini* swimsuit because I doubted there would be any time to swim at this late hour—and of course, there were no ladies' toilets or changing rooms at a beach as remote as Darak. Mohamed locked the car, and we hiked half an eternity through the sand towards the clashing waves of the Gulf of Oman.

On the way, we passed lagoons full of colorful seashells and sand dunes as tall as houses, as well as the legendary lone date palm in the sand. I was enchanted by the unfathomable beauty of Darak Beach and enjoyed every breath of air in this special place. That was, until Mohamed interrupted me . . .

"Take off your *hijab*, you don't need it here," he said, while attempting to open the brooch that kept my *dupatta* fixed around my head.

"Leave it, I don't want to take it off," I hastily replied, in shock at this sudden move.

"Don't worry, there are no people around, just you and I. Nobody will report you to the police here."

I tried to push him away, but it was too late—he had successfully removed my scarf and long, dark brown strands of hair were freely flowing in all directions.

"*Masha'Allah*, your hair is so beautiful!" Mohamed whispered as he ogled at me from all directions.

I felt violated. For many tourists, *hijab* is a mere legality when traveling in the Islamic Republic of Iran. It is mandated by law for women to cover their hair in public places to avoid arrest or worse. Hence, many visitors do not mind removing their scarves when nobody is watching, especially if they are not used to covering up in their home country. For me, however, *hijab* had a much deeper meaning. The long clothes that covered my body and the scarf around my head were my only protection—protection from the evil eye, which in this instance meant quite literally a pair of eyes with evil intentions.

I hated the thought processes that went through my head then, but in a society where a piece of cloth determines the honor, character, and respectability of a woman in men's eyes, I felt like observing *hijab* was the easiest way for me to signal that I was a "good girl" and unavailable for any man's immoral pleasures. Unfortunately, I learned quickly that these superficial efforts did little to change the preconceived opinions people held. If a man is so eager to strip a woman of her honor, character, respectability, and personhood, why would he not strip her of her headscarf as well? No matter how much effort a woman put into protecting herself, it was never enough. If she said "no," she was not dressed decently; if she was covered from head to toe, she was out alone; if she went out with her father, brother, and husband, she was still outside;

if she was inside her room, she did not lock the door properly. As a seasoned solo female traveler, I had known these things all too well, but I still tried to cling onto every yard of hope—the longer the scarf, the better. The fact that a strange man could have the audacity to touch a piece of clothing so sacred in the local context still deeply unsettled me. No man should ever force a woman to remove her *hijab*, no matter what her motivation behind wearing it is.

Angrily, I followed Mohamed to the waterfront, though I felt relieved he did not do worse things to me. I figured out that explaining to a grown-up Muslim man why removing a woman's headscarf is wrong would be pointless, so I instead focused my remaining energy on making the best out of my time in this paradisiac place. I took off my *sawas*, and with all my remaining clothes on, I carefully waded into the warm sea until I was immersed up to my shoulders. The warm evening sun shone directly in my face as I gently pushed myself forward against the currents, which thoroughly cleaned every last bit of clay from the fine stitches of my *dooch*. Through the clear water, I watched my bare feet as they were dancing with all the small crabs and algae that called Darak Beach their home. Meanwhile my mind drifted off into another world—a world where men truly respected women.

My train of thought was interrupted as a dark silhouette on a motorcycle emerged from behind the dunes. I quickly got out of the water and wrapped my *dupatta* back around my head, while Mohamed also turned around to see who was there. The dark figure parked his motorcycle in the sand and moved closer, until I clearly saw the face of a young, bearded man with a damp cloth wrapped around his head. He sat down on one of the taller dunes near the water and stared straight out into the sea. Coincidentally, we fell directly into his field of view.

It was at this point that the sickle-shaped half-moon emerged from the rapidly darkening sky, which had taken on a pinkish-violet tone. There was clearly no chance that we would make it back to Tis before dark, so I suggested we stay to watch this magical sunset, which brought out yet the best of Darak Beach. Mohamed, however, dismissed my idea.

"We should leave now," he said with an unusual sense of urgency in his voice.

"Let's stay for another ten minutes," I pleaded.

After traveling all the way to Darak, how could I possibly miss out on the best of this incredible golden hour?

"No, we must leave *now*," Mohamed replied sternly.

As we made our way back to the car, I noticed the strange man got back on his motorcycle and made a few large circles across the beach, passing by us a couple of times. Just a coincidence? *Maybe.* Mohamed doubled his walking pace and I followed suit.

When we finally reached our car, the man on the motorcycle pulled up next to us and greeted us in strange words. Mohamed signaled me to get into the car while he would handle the matter. Without saying a word, I got in and waited. The man on the motorcycle eventually rode off and Mohamed got into the driver's seat, started the engine, steered onto the road, and quickly drove off.

"What did he say?" I asked.

"I'll tell you later, let's get out of here first."

I bit my teeth as we raced through the red-tinted desert date plantations at 150 kilometers per hour. Freely roaming camels no longer seemed to be Mohamed's greatest concern at this point, and neither were his unsolicited advances to me. He was worried about something else, and I could not tell what it was.

When we reached the mountainous section of the road, Mohamed finally lifted his foot off the gas pedal and sighed in relief.

"What was that all about?" I impatiently asked.

Mohamed took a breath and explained, "That man was a robber . . . he had been watching us the entire time because he assumed we were Persians . . . because of my clothing. When we went to our car, he asked me for directions in Farsi, but I replied in Balochi and told him we're from here."

He sighed again and continued, "Robberies are very common in remote places here. He was just waiting for it to get dark, then he would have robbed us of every penny and maybe done even worse. I made sure to let him know I'm a local, though, and that I knew what he was up to."

I sat next to him in silence. *First, I nearly drowned in a mud volcano, then we got hunted down by a robber in the middle of nowhere; what other adventures will I experience alongside this creepy driver?* Knowing that at least we were safe now, I tried to direct my attention at the stunning blue hour that turned the rugged mountains around us into dark silhouettes, and uncovered thousands of stars in the lavender-colored sky. Unfortunately, these blissful moments were short-lived, because Mohamed soon began to bother me again.

"I really like you," he said with a soft smile.

I responded with a cold glare.

"I have a crush on you," he went on.

I added a hard eye roll to my glare.

"What a pity you are taken. If you had been single, I would have gone *inside* you today."

Upon hearing this, I nearly choked on the tea I had been sipping. I suddenly felt an intense urge to slap Mohamed across his face with my muddy *sawas*, but instead, I only let out an outraged "*astaghfirullah*" to express my disgust at his comment.

Noticing he had overstepped his boundaries way too much, Mohamed broke out into an embarrassed laughter and hastily replied, "Oh no, you misunderstood! Sorry, my English isn't good; I wanted to say something else. What did you think I was referring to?"

My unamused glare was sufficient to answer his question.

"Of course, I would never suggest *that*! I'm happily married to my gorgeous wife."

Bullcrap. He meant *exactly* what he had said. No translation error could bastardize a sentence's meaning this much.

Shortly after, Mohamed asked, "Do you know the police number in Iran?" he asked.

A chill ran down my spine. Why did he bring up the police? What was he up to? But most importantly, I realized that I did *not* know the local police number (which turned out to be 110, as in most countries). Afraid to admit my ignorance, I replied "yes" and vowed to myself to Google the number as soon as I got access to a mobile network. In the meantime, I recited a hundred prayers for my safety during this scary journey.

Ironically, only a few kilometers ahead, we neared an informal police checkpoint, and I watched Mohamed as he broke into a sweat. He hit the brake, slowly passed by the police cars, and sped off along the dark road, without regard for the camels that were allegedly the greatest danger in this section.

"Thank God, they didn't stop us! Sometimes police here block roads at night in remote areas to ask for bribes or, even worse, loot travelers," Mohamed explained.

Well, if the police here behave like this, maybe it's a good thing I don't know the emergency number. I felt a little better about myself after hearing this.

"All kinds of things happen here because Balochistan is so neglected." Mohamed's words reminded me of similar sentiments across the border on the Pakistani side.

"We are the poorest, least developed, and least educated province in Iran. Nobody in Tehran cares about what happens here. Many of them probably don't even know we exist." I could hear the pain in his voice.

Ironically, I was impressed when I first crossed the border and found running water, air-conditioning, and reliable electricity in the village. If this is the least developed region of Iran, how would the Pakistani side, where even the wealthiest households lack these basic amenities, compare on a larger scale?

"Of course, the authorities don't care about us because many of us are Sunni here. Iran is for Shia only."

Mohamed recounted stories of discrimination he faced based on ethnicity and religion. His experiences mirrored those of many minorities I had met around the world, but it hurt every time a person faced hostility because of factors that were outside of their control. Listening to these stories, I felt bad for his people, his family… heck, I almost even felt bad for him, but then I remembered this creep did not deserve any of my sympathy. Because of him, I was still in fear and my body was still shaking. All I could do was pray for him to get me back to Moslem's place unharmed.

To my relief, we crossed the camel road without further incidents and except for clumsy attempts to hold hands, Mohamed did nothing too disturbing. My tachycardia eventually subsided once I recognized the "I love Tis" sign in the dark, and I knew I was close to home.

As we entered the village, Mohamed turned towards me and said with a heavy sigh, "I realized you're not at all like a Western girl. You're just like a Baloch girl."

"What do you mean?" I replied, audibly annoyed. I knew exactly what he meant.

"You don't like touch," he dryly responded. "Even when we were climbing up the volcano, I tried to give you my hand, but you refused. A Baloch girl would have done the same."

"How do you think Western girls are different?" I asked.

"I know Western girls are very different. They're much more open-minded and enjoy having sex with strangers," he confidently claimed. "But you're not like a Western girl at all! I think you've spent too much time in Pakistan. The women there are similar to our Baloch girls."

I sighed. Having traveled extensively across Pakistan and the Middle East throughout the past years, I had far too often fallen victim to the awful stereotype of the "loose Western woman." With their only exposure to Western women through Hollywood films, music videos, or, worse, pornographic material, large numbers of men believed Western women were by default perpetually hungry for sex and hence, "easy to get." Using a false understanding of different cultural norms in the West, many men justified harassing Western women. Few realized that neither the normalization of casual sex nor the liberal dress code prevalent in many Western cultures replaced a woman's consent. Media loves to sensationalize short skirts and the adventurous sex lives of some women in the West, but it rarely shows women who decline a man's proposal. Given how widespread this phenomenon was and how few foreigners visited Balochistan, could I even blame Mohamed for his gross misunderstanding?

I took a deep breath and tried to educate Mohamed without letting my frustration spiral out of control.

"Not all Western women are like that," I began. "There are many modest women in Europe and America who don't participate in hookup culture and extramarital affairs. In fact, there are also many religious women in the West. Just like Islam, Christianity, and other religions also advocate for modesty and restraint."

A memory at the back of my mind interrupted my speech. I had once met a single, middle-aged woman who traveled the world solo and had romantic and sexual relations nearly everywhere she visited. Most certainly, she would have been considered "loose" in many contexts. Yet, she also entrusted me with harrowing stories of unwanted advances from men and her intense emotional reactions to these incidents reminded me of my own. She may have been "open-minded," "loose," or however one might want to phrase it, but that did not change the fact she also got sexually harassed just like me.

I quickly corrected myself and added, ". . . and even if a woman has casual sex with someone, it doesn't mean she would do the same with every man she meets. Consent is what matters."

Mohamed responded with a belittling smile. I could not tell if he took my words seriously or if he even listened to me at all. I hoped he did. I hoped that if he ever happened to meet a Western woman again, he would not make assumptions about her character or intentions based on her origin. A woman should not have to spend years living in a conservative society to say "no" to a man. Rejecting a man's advances does not make a woman Baloch but an autonomous human being. Still, I did not know if in Mohamed's mind I was still a Baloch girl or if I had achieved the status of a Western girl who simply did not want to be touched by every man.

Fortunately, the ordeal of this day trip finally came to an end when we pulled into Moslem's driveway and parked the car. Mohamed had invited me to come home with him to "meet my wife and kid" but naturally, I declined the offer. I paid him the agreed-upon amount plus a small tip, gathered my belongings, and exited his black, dusty car. As soon as he drove off, I blocked him on WhatsApp and ignored his numerous calls and text messages to my local number.

Back at Moslem's place, I received good news. In two days, a bus to Kerman would be available. Although this city was not part of my original itinerary, I was relieved to have finally found a way out of Chabahar and into the heart of Iran. I quickly confirmed the ticket, and the following day, I returned Moslem's wife's black *chadar* and moved out of their home to spend the last day with two boys that Jalal had connected me with. They were decent boys from a good family who would respect their guest and extend Balochi hospitality, Jalal assured me. However, with the trauma of the previous day still looming over me, I grew increasingly anxious while waiting for the boys to arrive. After all that had happened, how could I just trust these two strangers? What were the chances they, too, would judge my character based on my origin or the fact that I was traveling alone? Perhaps Jalal was right, the Baloch men of Iran could not be trusted, but then why did he entrust them with me?

Sure, there was no way for him to guess my concerns. I had not told anyone about my horrible experience with the taxi driver—neither Jalal, nor Moslem and his family, nor anybody else. Like all the previous times a man harassed me, I felt too ashamed to speak up. I had no idea where this shame stemmed from as I was not the one who did anything wrong, but perhaps I subconsciously did blame myself. After all, I could have protected myself by taking precautions. *Who advised me to travel alone to a remote place with a private driver when my host did not even let me go for a walk in the village alone?* Never mind, I did ask people to accompany me but they were all busy, which is why I went alone. *But then why did I still decide to go? I could have just stayed in and skipped Darak Beach.* Whatever. What was done was done.

Of course, looking back I realize that all I did was stay true to my mission, which I clung on to so tightly at the beginning of this journey: to face all the challenges that came with solo female travel to prove to the world women are capable of anything; but at the time, my confidence began to crumble.

After nearly two hours of anxiously waiting, the roars of a loud engine sounded from behind the wall, disrupting my train of thoughts. The boys had arrived! The two, whom I refer to as J&J due to their identical names, were both around the same age as me, if not a year or two younger, and seemed to belong to influential families. They dressed nearly identically, both sporting the Balochi version of the basic rich kid look with neatly ironed *shalwar kameez*, high-quality leather shoes, and expensive-looking branded watches. One of the boys spoke Urdu, the other one knew Farsi and Balochi only, so I communicated with him primarily through Google Translate. They welcomed me in their massive Toyota Land Cruiser, which reminded me a lot of Jalal's truck, and asked me to take a seat in the back. As we pulled out of the dusty driveway, the boys assured me they would take good care of my safety as Jalal had demanded of them.

With every minute I spent in the car without being touched or asked inappropriate questions, I gradually warmed up to the boys. They were kind and respectful, and despite the language barrier, their presence felt like a breath of fresh air compared to my previous experiences. After a delicious lunch at an upscale restaurant, J&J decided to take me to "their land": a collection of remote villages in the mountains north of Chabahar, where shepherds still lived in tent-like huts and drank from the skins of animals. I opened the windows to film the breathtaking landscape on the way but had to lower the shades whenever a car passed by because the boys' families' reputations would be harmed if they were seen in a car with a girl. Late at night, the two invited me to an underground party in one of their seaside mansions, where we danced to trending Balochi songs and the boys shared shot after shot of illegally imported whiskey—with lights off within soundproof walls so the police would not notice. After all, this was the Islamic Republic of Iran. And of course, the boys' parents knew nothing about the alcohol, the dancing, or the girl in their mansion. The same families that scrutinized every move of their daughters allowed their sons to roam around freely day and night. Nobody seemed to bother if their sons sinned, as long as they hid it—after all, they were not girls.

By the end of the night, I had grown quite comfortable around J&J. I was dancing inside a mansion with two intoxicated boys, but neither of them ever showed any ill intentions. They did not try to touch me or talk in a romantic manner, and they gave me the largest bedroom all to myself so I could rest peacefully. J&J assured me that they were both my hosts and friends; their actions affected not only themselves but also Jalal, who entrusted them to me. Furthermore, the fact that they drank alcohol in front of me, which they begged me to not tell anyone about, showed a great deal of mutual trust. Therefore, I decided to confide in them what had happened the day before.

"It's so unfair! Some men really believe they can do whatever they want with Western women," I concluded the story.

After apologizing on the behalf of the Baloch nation for what had happened on their land, J shared his thoughts with me. "I honestly don't think being a Westerner was the problem. Men do this to local girls as well."

The other J typed on his translator and showed it to me. "I think the main reason was that you were alone. People here believe that good girls don't go outside alone, and if a girl is all by herself, she must be a bad girl and they can do whatever they want to her."

I bit my tongue as I digested their opinions. They were harsh and sad, but unfortunately, sounded realistic.

"People here want to believe that they respect women, but in the end, they always do what they want anyway, and try to find reasons to justify their actions," J added.

By the time of this conversation, the first sun rays had begun to peak across the horizon, and I excused myself to go to sleep. I went inside the large bedroom and lay down in the soft, king-sized bed with mixed emotions. On the one hand, I felt grateful for this fun, relaxed, and safe day with J&J, as well as the cultural insights I gained from these open-minded young men. In many ways, I was reminded of my journey with Jalal and Sanaullah and relived the same careless, adventurous energy. For a day, I was "just like a man" again and it felt refreshing, liberating. On the other hand, I kept thinking about what the boys had just told me. It felt bitter to know that going out alone as a woman was considered reason enough to be harassed, and that people here would think of me as a "bad girl." Although I kept telling myself how wrong this notion was, I could not help but feel even more discouraged, and somehow this conversation even reinforced my earlier doubts. I used my *dupatta* to wipe away the tiny tears that were rolling down my cheek. I had just received a reality check and slowly began to think that perhaps traveling across Balochistan was not such a great idea after all.

Sometime around noon, J&J knocked on my door and told me to get ready quickly. My bus was scheduled to depart in the afternoon, and with so few routes available, I could not afford to miss it. It took me great effort to get out of the comfortable bed at such an early hour by post-party standards. J&J and I shared the leftover slices of kebab pizza from the previous night for breakfast and flushed it down with the last remaining drops of whiskey. Afterwards, I took a shower and got dressed, with the boys advising me what to wear for the journey. They picked out the least flashy *chadar* from my luggage and told me to take off all my jewelry. After all, I was traveling alone and had to take precautions.

J&J drove me to the bus terminal in the northern fringes of Chabahar. They guided me through the crowded waiting halls to the counter of the bus company that was arranging the trip to

Kerman. Then, it was time to say goodbye, and the boys left for their university, where they were scheduled to take an exam later in the day.

With my heavy luggage in tow, I gazed around the sweltering, crowded bus terminal and realized that, among all the families waiting for their buses, I was the only passenger sitting all by myself. At first, I was able to secure a seat on a hard bench, but when I had to go to the bathroom and returned, I could barely find a spot on the floor. Women of all ages gave me strange looks that I could not decipher, and eventually, an employee approached me and said something to me in Balochi. When he realized I could not understand him, he called over a colleague who was fluent in Urdu. Shocked to see a young woman sitting on the floor all alone, the man guided me into his company's office and told the men there to leave, so that I had a waiting room all to myself. He knocked on the door a few times to offer me water or tea, and eventually called me when my bus was ready to depart.

Some employees carried my luggage to the bus while I entered the air-conditioned vehicle and settled in my assigned seat. The bus belonged to a small, locally owned company, and was in relatively good condition for Balochistan standards,—which meant it was still very uncomfortable for a long-haul journey like the one ahead of me. My seat was barely cushioned and non-reclinable, and I mentally prepared myself for the stiff neck I would experience the following morning. The travel time from Chabahar to Kerman was estimated at somewhere between thirteen and fourteen hours—a long drive but still one of the shortest routes to make it out of this remote corner of the country. My phone was barely charged, and I did not have any food on me; what a bummer I did not buy a kebab sandwich when I had the chance! I looked around and realized the bus was completely full, except for the seat next to me, since strange men cannot be seated next to a woman. I was surrounded by scores of men and a few families in the back. Every single one of them was speaking Balochi; few outsiders seemed to come to Chabahar. Once everyone had settled down, I felt the wheels rolling underneath me as the bus pulled out of the parking lot. *This is it*, I thought. After nearly two weeks, I would finally make it out of this city and continue my dream journey to Persia.

With my phone in battery-save mode, my eyes were glued on the landscape beyond the window and the beautiful mountains that emerged as soon as we departed from Chabahar. We drove along the same road that J&J had taken me on the previous day but continued farther north. The views became more and more stunning by the minute, as mountains grew taller and more rugged, and the setting sun produced increasingly warm light. My mind became so fixated on the natural beauty in front of my eyes that I soon forgot about my surroundings inside this cramped bus. I was enchanted. A bittersweet feeling overcame me when I realized this would be my last sunset in Balochistan, and so were the memories that came to my mind. Balochistan was meant to be merely a transit zone on my journey to Tehran, but after all this time spent on this magnificent land, it had become much more to me. I felt that with every peak we passed, I left a tiny piece of my heart behind.

No matter how magical the moment, it was meant to be surpassed on the linear journey that is time. After roughly two hours on the road, the last shades of afterglow disappeared behind the mountains to the west and I witnessed the dazzling wonderland around us transform into a dark void, leaving nothing but the stars and our bus's headlights to illuminate the ravined road in front of us.

We were somewhere near Nikshahr when the bus pulled into a primitive rest area equipped with a small petrol pump, washrooms, a mosque, and a few tuck shops. Based on the driver's announcement, I understood we would spend only ten minutes in this rest area, and we would have a proper dinner break farther down the road. Following the passengers ahead of me, I gathered my valuables and haphazardly made my way out of the bus, trying not to trip over the *chadars* and long dresses of the women in the front. After taking my turn to use the dirtiest roadside washroom I had seen in my entire life (and that was *a lot*), I decided there was enough time for my regular black-tea fix. I felt proud when I walked into one of the tuck shops and ordered my tea by saying "*yak chai bide.*" All the Balochi I had learned from Mureed's family was coming to use now that I was by myself!

I tiptoed my way back to the bus, trying not to spill my hot tea, when I noticed a man staring me down from top to bottom. He was with two other men and looked like he wanted to say something to me. *Did I drop something?* I wondered. I covered my face and passed by the group expecting to hear a word from them, but they remained silent. When I sat down in my assigned seat, I noticed the three men sat in the rows across from me, with the staring man right across the aisle.

With nothing but darkness outside of my windows, I put in my earbuds and listened to the Balochi playlist that Umair had shared with me. I decreased my screen's brightness to minimum to preserve battery and scrolled through my chats and feeds a few times while there was still internet connection. I felt bored but not tired enough to sleep, hungry but without food for the next couple of hours, lonely but with no one to talk to. I tried everything to kill time, not an easy task when one is traveling all alone . . . was I really, though? In between my desperate attempts to distract my mind from the lack of mental stimulation around me, I could not help but feel as if I was being watched.

After about two hours, I tracked our location somewhere near Iranshahr when our bus finally pulled into a bigger rest area. *Finally, time for dinner*! I excitedly thought while getting out of my seat, fantasizing about whatever delicious meal I was going to devour throughout the next half an hour. I made my way past the staring man, whose eyes were, to my surprise, again fixated on me, and became one of the first to exit the bus. I was really that hungry!

Naan koja milli? Naan koja milli? In my head, I kept practicing the line that Sanaullah had taught me once to ask where I could find food. There were various buildings around me that looked like they could be restaurants—but also could be something entirely different. Given that gender-segregated dining halls were the norm in this part of the world, I decided to approach a family to ask for the dining hall.

I cleared my throat and nervously repeated the phrase, "*Naan koja milli*?"

Without blinking an eye, the women pointed towards the large building in front of us. I thanked them and briskly made my way to the dining hall.

I silently settled down at the first table I could find. It was covered in rice grains and grease spots, but I did not mind; I just wanted to eat. To my surprise, this dining hall was not segregated by gender, and I was the only woman in a room full of men—nothing I was not used to, but it still made me feel uncomfortable. *Control your nerves, it's just a dinner*, my inner voice urged me, so I leaned back in my chair and waited for the waiter to approach me.

Five minutes passed. I watched the young boy working at this restaurant as he paced from table to table taking orders and serving food but always walking right past me. *Perhaps I should call him over*, I thought, still not quite familiar with the local dining customs. I raised my arm and waved at the boy; he noticed me and walked over.

"*Che naan aste*?" I asked for the menu.

The boy replied and I understood they only had chicken with rice. I asked him to bring me a plate of chicken and rice, to which he nodded and paced to the kitchen, yelling out the order.

While waiting for my dish with a grumbling stomach, I watched the men around me as they gave orders, received their food, and finished their plates within minutes, yet I continued to starve. *Why is my order taking so long?* I wondered. *I ordered the same thing as everyone else; this doesn't make sense.* I continued to wait calmly, without too much concern. I told myself we were only ten minutes into the break, there should be enough time to finish my meal, use the washroom, and make it back to the bus on time. *Probably the waiter just forgot about me*, I thought. I waved at the boy again and repeated my order. Again, he took note and went to the kitchen.

Another five minutes passed, and I gradually became annoyed. More and more men had entered the hall, ordered food, ate, and left, but I was still waiting. It felt as if I lost a fraction of patience every time my heart pumped more glucose-deprived blood through my veins. I was really hungry! On the benches outside of the restaurant, a little girl from the family I had talked to earlier noticed something was wrong and ran into the dining hall.

She approached the young waiter and told him something along the lines of: "Please bring this lady some food, she's been waiting for a long time."

The boy nodded and ran back to the kitchen, yelling the order. Same words, nothing changed.

In the meantime, two more men entered the hall. I recognized them as my bus driver and his assistant. They sat down two tables away from me and gave their orders to the young boy, who had come to their service within seconds. Over the next ten minutes, I watched the boy relay the order to the kitchen staff and serve the meals to the men, the men finish their meals, and the boy clear their tables. I had reminded him once or twice more in between, but again nothing happened.

Meanwhile, the bus driver and his assistant shot a few brief glances in my direction that increased in frequency throughout their meal. Unlike the staring man's stares, their glances had no unsettling energy to them, only impatience. They knew the clock was ticking and, in a few minutes, we were scheduled to resume our journey. They also knew I was their passenger and had been waiting for my meal all this time. As they handed over their cash to the young boy, they gestured towards me and spoke to him in harsh words. And voilà! A few seconds later, like a miracle, my steaming hot plate of chicken with rice was finally in front of me!

Frustrated by this long wait but relieved my food had eventually arrived, I picked up some rice with my hand and formed it into a ball, just like Mureed's daughters had taught me. Finally, I would get to replenish my exhausted energy reserves, I thought. However, just as I was about to open my mouth, I overheard the driver yell impatiently at the waiter, who quickly rushed into the kitchen and handed me a Styrofoam box. It was clear that we were running late, and the driver wanted me to pack my food and eat it on the bus. I shoved the layers of saffron-infused basmati rice into the box, paid the waiter, and followed the driver back to the bus. And with little surprise at this point, as I made my way to my seat, the man across the aisle stared at me again.

I sat down in my seat and placed the Styrofoam box on my lap. My stomach was still grumbling but by this point my frustration had outgrown my hunger. Before touching any of my food, I pulled out my phone to reply to messages while there was still mobile reception around Iranshahr. Sanaullah happened to be online at the time, so I decided to vent to him about my experience at the restaurant.

"It really seemed like the boy understood me, he even confirmed my order with the kitchen! How can language barrier cause such problems?" I complained to Sanaullah in simple Urdu.

His response, however, was different from what I had expected.

"What illiterate idiots, I can't believe they did this to you!" Sanaullah's texts sounded even angrier than mine.

"It's not because of the language barrier, they clearly understood you. It's because you were alone! They don't take women seriously without a man!" he wrote.

After reading this text, it all suddenly made sense to me, and I was overcome by the same depressing feeling I experienced after my conversation with J&J the night before. As a woman all by myself, nobody heard me. My voice was just as meaningless to them as the little girl's, which was ignored alongside mine. Only after the bus driver, a man, spoke up, did they finally listen and do their work. They served me, but under a man's command. My mind went off on involuntary tangents again, blaming myself for the treatment I received and calling myself a "bad girl" for being out on the road all by myself. I felt terrible.

All the while, the hearty fragrance of the grilled chicken inside my Styrofoam box rose into my nostrils, triggering my primal human feeding response, but I no longer felt hungry. Something in my head was blocking the natural urge to eat. I buried the box under my seat alongside the humiliating feeling of nonexistence and tried to forget about it.

It was already well into the night, and I shut my eyes in an attempt to fall asleep, but no matter how hard I tried, it felt impossible. Something was keeping me up, but I could not tell what it was. There was no light, no noise, and the road wasn't bumpy; perhaps it was my hypoglycemia, although I really did not think it was. I sat cramped up in my double seat, muscles tense and shivering, although it was not cold; my mouth was dry and I could hear my heartbeat despite wearing earbuds. I felt uneasy and unable to relax—hallmarks of the fight-or-flight response, the involuntary release of adrenaline when one's body senses danger. But how could I have been in danger? I was sitting safely in the seat of a bus, surrounded by dozens of families and a driver who was kind enough to order food on my behalf. Everything seemed fine.

Nonetheless, something felt off. It was the same odd feeling of being watched that I had sensed earlier. I turned around, and across the aisle sat the staring man, with his heavy body crouched over his seat and his big blue-green eyes bulging out of his skull. He was going out of his way to watch me with no intentions to hide it, which was never a good sign.

Trying to convey my discomfort without words, I adjusted my *chadar* to properly cover my hands, mouth, nose, and hairline, leaving only my eyes exposed. *See, I'm a good girl, I'm covering up, I'm hiding, I don't want to be seen by you, I don't want to tempt you*, my dress screamed—but to no avail. The staring man did not take his eyes off me or, better put, my fabric. With the majority of passengers sleeping, he had nothing to lose; it almost felt as if we were in private. I now understood why my body did not let me sleep. With the last watchful pair of eyes gone inside the bus, this man would have been free to do whatever he wanted.

The next couple of hours were pure dread. I hated sitting alone in the darkness with nothing to do, unable to sleep, and a disgusting man who seemingly felt no remorse for his behavior. I did not notice when we crossed the provincial border between Sistan and Baluchestan and Kerman, but I remember we were somewhere near Bam when our bus stopped for its last break. *Bam, the city of sweet dates*, I recalled, although my memories of eating Bam dates next to Mohamed were not sweet at all. I felt relieved when our bus pulled up across from a public washroom at the terminal. My bladder could barely hold onto its contents as I'd had no time for a washroom stop during our last break.

I made my way out of the bus, and the staring man and his companions trailed behind me. Our paths split as I walked into the ladies' side and they entered the gentlemen's side, but when I came out a few minutes later, they were standing in front of me, waiting. There were no other people around us as most passengers were asleep, and the path towards the bus was pitch-dark. The man continued staring creepily while I walked towards the bus as briskly as possible. Then, when I was halfway into the dark zone, my heart stopped. He spoke to me! I did not understand what he said, but from his behavior I could tell his intentions were not good.

Perhaps it was wrong to not ignore him. These men are desperate for attention and, with any reaction, no matter how snarky, a woman gives in to this demand. However, I could not stay silent after he had been disturbing my peace for so many hours.

I angrily snapped back at him, "*Che*?"

This word translates to "what" in English, but in my mind, the meaning was much closer to: "LEAVE ME THE FUCK ALONE, I KNOW WHAT YOU'RE UP TO, YOU FILTHY DOG!"

Fortunately, it was at this moment that we entered the field of view of the driver's assistant, and noticing this additional pair of eyes, the men quickly dispersed and acted as if nothing had happened. Typical *tharki* behavior.

The remaining two hours on this bus were uneventful. As before, most passengers remained asleep. I squeezed against the window even though my double seat gave me plenty of space. I just wanted to get as far away as possible from the staring man, who continued with his repulsive behavior throughout the rest of the journey. I could not see the first sun rays of the day as we were driving west; but I knew they were hiding somewhere behind the mountains in the east as they slowly transformed the dark sky into lighter shades of blue. I was confident the day had already begun in Balochistan. Soon enough in Lasbela, Jalal's daughters would wake up to another day spent within their four walls. In the village, another young girl would get her ears pierced with thread and needle in preparation for her marriage to a man twice her age. And in Chabahar, Mohamed's wife would rise early to diligently prepare breakfast for her husband, unaware of how many other women he would touch that day. This morning, millions of "good girls" would wake up across Balochistan to serve their fathers, brothers, husbands, and sons. They would do what women were supposed to do. Meanwhile, here I was, a "bad girl" traveling all alone with no regard for my honor, inviting all the bad treatment that I apparently deserved. Sure enough, I had begun to feel the consequences of trying to act "just like a man." I should not have defied the rules for Baloch girls.

I melancholically leaned my fully covered head against the window and listened to the monotone sound of the tires rolling rapidly across the asphalt. I was now finally in Persia, on my way to pursue a lifelong dream and explore the majestic culture, history, and architecture of a Middle Eastern treasure chest, but all I could think of were the life-altering encounters of the past two weeks. After having traveled to hundreds of places around the world, why did this transit region have such a profound impact on me? What power did this place possess to prompt me to question my very own identity? Did I discover the universal truth about gender relations and femininity in Balochistan? My experiences throughout the past two weeks made me wonder if God truly did design women to be inherently different from men, with different roles, responsibilities, and places to be. Perhaps the people of Balochistan were merely following the natural order and it was me, the Westerner, who had been led astray by too many bad influences. Within the blessings of their homes, the Baloch women I met were mastering the arts of cooking and embroidery, henna and beautification, bearing sons to continue the bloodline and raising daughters to pass on traditions. Outside, however, their excellence was as hidden as their faces. Either to shelter them from the harsh sunlight and the shrill sounds of gun shots, or to foster a sense of masculinity in their men, I could not tell. But I knew that if they transgressed this order, there would be punishment, maybe from their family or from strangers or from God. And more likely than not, my bad experiences were well-deserved punishment, I thought. If so, could I ever continue my mission as a solo female traveler with a clear conscience? Or was I meant to give it all up and aim to live an honorable, feminine life?

With thousands of conflicting thoughts racing through my head, I directed my gaze at the ever more recognizable outlines of the road outside of the window. The bus was traveling so fast that the bright markings on the asphalt appeared to be blurred into continuous lines. This came to no surprise, considering we were covering the nearly thousand kilometers between Chabahar and Kerman in a single night. I came to the realization that with every passing second, I was leaving farther and farther behind the land that had given me so many beautiful memories alongside heartbreaking realizations. Physically, that is. Mentally, I had not moved an inch.

CHAPTER SIX

INTO ANOTHER WORLD

Slowly but eventually, the sun made her way beyond the eastern peaks and painted the surrounding peaks in a soft red color. The mountains of Kerman appeared distinct from the mountains of Balochistan. They were smaller, less rugged, and brighter in color, kind of like sugar cubes compared to rock candy. From then on, it was only a short drive to the bus terminal of Kerman City, marking the end of this dreadful thirteen-hour journey. The staring man gave me one last intense look as we got off the bus but was fortunately interrupted by the bus driver's assistant, who shot him a threatening glance while unloading the baggage. Then, we finally parted ways.

The moment I stepped out of the bus alongside the scores of *dooch-* and *shalwar-kameez*-clad women and men, I felt like I had entered another world. A world where the air tasted chalkier and dry heat scratched my skin. I had traveled nearly a thousand kilometers inland and was surrounded by an arid desert that made days scorching and nights freezing—no more "four springs" as in Chabahar. However, what truly made this world different was not its geography but its people. Suddenly, people around me spoke Farsi instead of Balochi; women wore fashionable tunics and short scarves instead of heavy embroidered dresses and black *chadars*; men wore dress shirts and pants instead of *shalwar kameez*; their faces were cleanly shaven with no long hair or beards; men and women were waiting for their buses alone or in couples instead of in large family groups; they carried themselves with confidence and independence instead of with modesty and restraint. In short, they were the opposite of everything I had gotten used to over the past two weeks.

At first, I felt a sense of safety around the people who I had learned to emulate throughout the past two weeks. However, as more and more of my fellow passengers from Chabahar gradually trickled out of the vast parking lot, I found myself in a foreign world surrounded by people who seemed inherently different from "us." I wished I could have joined one of the many Baloch families who climbed into taxis bound for unknown destinations, but I had to wait. My host was on his way to pick me up and take me to his home at the other end of the city.

I knew Mehdi from Couchsurfing, an international platform that connects travelers looking for a place to stay with locals willing to host a traveler in their homes for cultural exchange. I had searched the app the previous evening in a last-minute attempt to find a host for a night in Kerman. Mehdi instantly accepted my request as he was excited to meet a foreigner in his city. Our acquaintanceship was just as spontaneous as my plan to visit Kerman, which was why I felt even more grateful that he woke up before sunrise to pick me up at this early hour.

My previous self would have just booked a hotel with twenty-four-hour reception, but this option did not even come to my mind this time. I forgot that single women were allowed to rent rooms in most parts of the world, and not everywhere was it as challenging to travel alone as a woman as in Balochistan. Without any other options, staying at local people's homes had become the norm for me there, and it was no challenge in a place where social circles were tightly knit, in any given town or village everyone knew someone, and a deeply rooted culture of hospitality made welcoming strangers into one's home an everyday occurrence. Persia, however, was different. Few of my Baloch acquaintances knew any Persians, and vice versa. It seemed like the two peoples lived in separate worlds. So, unable to stay with one of Jalal's acquaintances from now on, there was only one logical option: Couchsurfing.

About half an hour later, Mehdi rolled up in front of me in a silver Toyota. The sleepy-eyed skinny young man welcomed me by helping me carry my luggage to his vehicle and asked me to get in the front seat. After apologizing and thanking him a dozen times for arriving at this early hour of the day, we introduced ourselves to each other. As his nerdy appearance suggested, Mehdi was a computer programmer in his late twenties and, like most people in Kerman, Persian by ethnicity. When it was my turn, I told him about myself and the places I had visited in the last two weeks.

"Oho! Balochistan very dangerous!" he exclaimed in broken English.

He inspected me from head to toe with his mouth wide open, probably wondering how a girl like me had made it across Balochistan all alone.

Not sure how to react to his remark, I responded with a polite giggle. Mehdi's geeky but relaxed aura was slightly awkward but I felt comfortable sitting next to him in the front seat, unlike during my day trip with Mohamed. Our conversation was not particularly lively, but I felt safe.

A drive across the city later, we rolled into the neat underground garage of a high-rise apartment building. Mehdi passed me my suitcase from the trunk, which I dragged across the smooth concrete floor into an elevator that led directly to his apartment. I felt like my muscles had gotten weak during the two weeks in which I had not lifted any weight, but at least I did not have to deal with bumpy dirt roads here. I followed Mehdi inside his small apartment, which he shared with his brother.

"My brother and I sleep here, but you can go in that room over there," he explained as we passed by a pair of mattresses in the living room.

Upon entering a small bedroom, he apologized. "I'm sorry, there's no space in the wardrobe because my girlfriend's clothes are there. She stays over every other night."

"That's fine, I'll be here for one night only," I replied, hiding my astonishment.

Girlfriend? Sleeping over? That would be unheard of in Balochistan!

I rested my suitcase against the wall and went to the bathroom to take a shower. After I returned to the room, Mehdi knocked on the door and announced, "My brother and I are leaving for work now. We'll be back in the evening. Feel free to take anything from my fridge but make sure to close the door properly. Also, make sure all taps are closed as not to waste any water. Oh, and if you want to do some sightseeing, I recommend you head directly to the main bazaar and . . ."

Before he could finish his sentence, I interrupted him. "I don't think that's possible. I'm alone, there's no one I can go sightseeing with."

Mehdi responded with a puzzled look. "So what? How does that prevent you from sightseeing?"

"I—I'm a woman!" I stuttered.

"That's not a problem. It's very safe here," Mehdi assured me, seemingly unable to comprehend my hesitation.

"But women don't just roam around alone here, do they?" I asked, confused.

"Of course, they do!" Mehdi replied, audibly irritated. "I know the Western media paints a certain picture of Iranian women, but don't fall for it, it's not the reality."

His response surprised me. "It's not about the Western media," I replied. "It's . . . the reality in Balochistan."

Mehdi went on to give me tips for exploring Kerman. He instructed me to download a local rideshare app, which allowed me to swiftly arrange rides from A to B. Then, without further ado, he and his brother headed out of the apartment, leaving behind a spare key so I could return to the apartment later.

Choosing my clothes that day was not an easy task. *I'm no longer in Balochistan, I can finally wear the other half of my clothes that are not* pashk, I thought. I pulled dress after dress out of my suitcase but could not settle on anything—one looked too Western, one too Pakistani. What does one even wear in Persia?

I ended up wearing a relatively plain, dark-colored set of ladies' *shalwar kameez* I had bought from a village bazaar in northern Pakistan. As for my head covering, I did not want to wear the beautiful embroidered *chadar* Jalal's family had gifted me, neither did I want to wear anything else that looked visibly foreign. Recalling the images of the modern Persian women I had seen at the bus station, I selected a short, light *dupatta.* It was deep yellow with a colorful floral print, one of the beautiful designs that had caught my attention on a trip to Kurdistan. I pinned up my long, dark hair in a bun and wrapped the scarf loosely around my head. *Just like a Persian girl*, I thought.

Like Mehdi had suggested, I used the rideshare app to arrange a car to the main bazaar. A short drive later, a bustling market street emerged from the ocean of residential buildings that was lined with shop after shop selling everything from textiles to spices. The structure and architecture of this market was vastly different from the chaotic, open-air collections of street stalls and textile shops in Balochistan or Pakistan; its square-shaped plazas and endless covered market halls much more resembled the traditional bazaars of Kurdistan. I followed the driver's suggestion and exited the car at a busy intersection.

As soon as I got out, I found myself immersed in a colorful crowd of women and men, girls, and boys. I took careful steps in the direction of the flow and was overtaken by dozens of fashionable young women who confidently roamed the street alone. In a way, it reminded me of Western Europe, where I grew up, yet I stared at the women as if it was my first time seeing this. Amazed by a concept so familiar but suddenly foreign, I followed the crowd until I had almost caught up with the other women. Walking across the bustling streets of the old city of Kerman felt daunting at first but eventually liberating.

The flow of shoppers led me inside a large, noisy market hall with hundreds of shops side by side—think Istanbul's Grand Bazaar minus the tourist crowds. I looked around this colorful hall like a child lost in an art gallery. Everything seemed so different, so foreign to me that I barely paid attention to the items being sold. Unlike the people around me, I was not a shopper but merely an observer, a tourist.

Somewhere down the alley, my ears caught the distant beats of music in between all the yelling and chatter. I followed the beats until I reached a gate in the middle of the alley that led down a set of stairs. In the inscription above the entrance, I deciphered the word *hammam*—bathhouse. *Why is there music coming from a bathhouse?* I wondered. I knew that in old times, bathhouses in many places were open to only men. I was just about to walk on when a group of women entered in front of me, and curiosity urged me to follow suit.

When I reached the end of the staircase, I was surprised by what I found in front of me: a lively café with deafeningly loud live performances of traditional Persian music, filled with chanting and dancing crowds and the scent of tea and hookah steam in the air. Quickly, I figured out that the historic *hammam* of Kerman today served as a cultural gathering spot rather than a bathhouse, its original purpose. The real surprise, however, lay in the social dynamics of this place. There was no gender segregation whatsoever; women not only dined alongside men, but they also smoked, danced, and sang along; many had come with groups of friends rather than their families; there were no black *chadars* or heavy dresses in sight, only light scarves that loosely covered the backsides of women's heads; some women even removed their headscarves altogether, a crime in the Islamic Republic of Iran. I made my way through the celebrating masses to a table in the back that had a free seat and ordered a can of tea. The bittersweet taste of Iranian *chai* on my tongue provided temporary relief to the pain in my ear drums, and as I slowly stirred the rock-sugar stick in my cup, I kept thinking about how impossible such a place would be in Balochistan.

After emptying the last drop of tea from my can, I paid the bill and headed back to explore the market hall, still in awe of what I had just witnessed. Amidst the chaotic masses, I detected a familiar pattern: thick yet intricate embroidery on long colorful fabrics, engulfed by a large black cloth—I spotted a Baloch woman roaming the crowded streets with her husband and four children. I continued my stroll, but the more I paid attention, the more black *chadars* and *dooch* patterns I saw. Soon enough, I came to the realization that the vibrant market of Kerman invited a diverse crowd, and the number of Baloch families was not negligible.

Slowly but surely, my steps became heavier and self-conscious thoughts overwhelmed my mind. Were the sleeves of my *kameez* too short and my scarf too loose? Was my outfit too colorful? What if I, for some reason, stood out in this crowd? Were other shoppers staring at me? If so, for what reason? Certainly, I preferred to err on the side of caution. I stopped at a shop in the corner of the market hall and bought myself a black Irani chador—*better safe than sorry*, I thought.

I continued my stroll, covered from head to toe in a large black cloth. Unlike the *chadar* that Moslem's wife had lent me, this one had a rubber band to fix it above my head as well as very baggy sleeves that ensured my arms were covered properly. I instantly felt safer, more protected, and within my comfort zone. I continued my walk with light and modest steps, the ladylike gait that comes naturally when wearing a *chadar*. To my confusion, I now received more stares from the Baloch women in the market. They were not stares of shock and surprise but rather the knowing type of glance people exchange when they run into an acquaintance. Out of habit, I covered my face every time I walked past a man in *shalwar kameez*. Some of them, in particular those who were not with their families, turned around after me and stared just like the man on the bus, or at least I perceived it so.

As for the Persians, most women and men appeared rather distant yet courteous. Shopkeepers were not pushy and quoted me reasonable prices even though I could not speak Farsi. When I entered museums, the ticket vendors always charged me the lower entrance fees for Iranians instead of the higher foreigner rate. One vendor would not even believe me when I tried to explain to her I was from abroad. "You look Zahedani;" or "I thought you were from the southeast," many people I talked to told me. I could not understand why they thought this—I was not even wearing *dooch*!

——— ··•·· ———

At the end of my very long first day in Persia, I hailed a taxi back to Mehdi's place and climbed up to his apartment, exhausted. When Mehdi opened the door, his jaw dropped in shock.

"You look . . . very dangerous! Like terrorist!" he exclaimed in a horrified tone.

Taken aback by his comment, I did not know how to respond. I walked past him, went straight to my room, and stared at myself in the mirror for a good ten minutes. In front of me was the silhouette of a short young woman, covered from head to toe in black cloth, leaving only my pale hands and blueish-green eyes exposed. I was in shock. Not because of the way I looked—I looked like any other woman I had seen over the past few weeks. Rather, it was Mehdi's comment that shocked me. How could he be afraid of all the women who housed me, fed me, looked out for me, and shared their precious affection with me over the past weeks? How could anyone liken such warm, gentle human beings to terrorists? What wrong had they done to the world? I recalled the time at Darya Bozorg when I attracted stares for wearing a colorful *chadar*. Now, the opposite was happening! Mehdi's comment was yet another slap in the face of a girl with already badly damaged self-esteem. I had tried so hard to blend in, to be accepted and respected by the people around me, just to be rejected by the next group of people. Was I never good enough?

I fought to hold back my tears as I stared in the mirror trying to come up with things to blame myself for, but then I remembered that all this self-deprecating thinking was but a waste of time. The reality was that I was still traveling, in the middle of my dream journey, and as a traveler I had to adapt. I had adapted well enough to the culture of Balochistan to survive, but now it was time to let go of all I had learned over the past two weeks and change myself all over again. Not an easy task even after years on the road, but what else could I do but try? I had to accept that I was now in a different world, with different people and different rules, a world so close yet so far from the one I had just left behind.

The patterns of shock, surprise, and gradual learning only kept repeating themselves as I continued my journey. Over the following days, I traveled from Kerman to Yazd, then to Shiraz, Persepolis, Esfahan, and Qom. The backache from the accumulated long hours spent on intercity buses and the accompanying sleep deprivation were mild in comparison to the wide cultural disparities I encountered. While the majority of people I met in Qom were closest to the people of Balochistan in terms of their conservative mindsets and religiosity, many others held beliefs that could not contrast more with the ones I had gotten used to during my time in Balochistan. Some tour guides bragged about being atheists, others criticized my modest choice of clothing, claiming it supported the visions of an oppressive regime. I had hosts who invited me for shots of hard liquor and organized rave parties in the desert. The men who guided me through the Zoroastrian Towers of Silence in Yazd reminisced about ancient Persia before the introduction of Islam and openly expressed their contempt for the religion that they felt had been forced onto them by the government. Just about everyone seemed more approving of the mingling of genders than in Balochistan, but I was pleasantly surprised to find the majority of men very courteous and respectful—even taxi drivers!

As expected, whenever I mentioned my time in Balochistan, I was met with shock, followed by a cascade of negative stereotypes. "It's so dangerous, no Iranian would ever want to go there" and "people there are strange; they are very poor and uneducated and have no manners" were things I heard from almost every Persian I talked to. Usually, I would try to counter their claims with beautiful photos of the region and stories of incredible Balochi hospitality, although I remain doubtful about whether I successfully managed to change anyone's mind.

The incident from this leg of the trip that stood out to me the most happened during my overnight bus journey from Shiraz to Esfahan. It was very late, sometime between two and three o'clock in the morning. I had just dozed off in the relative comfort of my front-row seat, with my black *chador* draped over my tired face, exposing only the intricate *dooch* patterns of the Balochi dress I was wearing for this journey. All of a sudden, the vehicle stalled, and I abruptly woke up. We had just crossed the provincial border and were subjected to a routine inspection at a police checkpoint. After all my traveling in the country, this was nothing new to me. Police would simply stop the bus, take a quick glance inside, and then let it continue its journey. This time was different, however. Two police officers, one male and one female, entered the vehicle and pointed their flashlights across the cabin. Eventually, both beams fixated on my face. I quickly came to my senses as the bright light pierced my sleepy eyes. The police officers talked to me in Farsi, but all I could understand was their hand gestures, urging me to get off the bus. Confused, I followed their commands.

Once we were outside of the vehicle, they began questioning me. All I could understand was "*koja,*" which means "where" in both Balochi and Farsi. Were they asking me where I was coming from or where I was going? I was not sure, so I replied,

"Shiraz, Esfahan." Next, the officers requested to see my "*kart*," which I figured out meant my Iranian ID card. I pulled out my German passport and handed it to the lady, who was visibly puzzled. She stared at the red cover with her mouth wide open; then she erratically flipped through the pages before fixating on the information page featuring my hijab-less passport photo. After a while, she asked, "Passport Irani?"

I replied, "No, no, *almani, almani*!"

Upon hearing this, her expression changed from confusion to shock. She looked at the information page a couple more times to confirm that the person in the photo was indeed me. I showed her the printed page of my Iran visa. Finally, she seemed convinced my identity was real. She excitedly told her colleague "*Almani! Almani*!" and allowed me to return to the bus. No further check, no trouble, German tourists were apparently incapable of doing wrong.

The incident itself lasted less than five minutes and caused no delay to the bus's schedule, but the memory became etched into the back of my mind. Why was it that out of the dozens of people on board, the police asked only me to step out? What—in the minds of law enforcement—made me stand out as a potential criminal, victim, or any other person of concern? My main theory is that it was my clothing. Out of all the people wearing shirts and trousers, tunics and *dupattas*, I stood out as the only person in Balochi dress. When I recalled the experiences of ethnic and religious discrimination Mohamed had shared with me as well as all the negative stereotypes mentioned by the Persians I had met, I concluded this was the most probable explanation. Nearly 2000 kilometers to the west, someone traveling from the country's poorest and most underdeveloped province, riddled with unrest, and—most significantly—a distinct minority culture, may indeed become a subject of interest for law enforcement.

To be fair, I had little knowledge of the law-and-order situation across Iran, so I may have been unqualified to judge. On the one hand, I acknowledged that where there was poverty and unrest, other miseries would follow. Jalal had warned me many times of criminal activity in the border region between Pakistan and Iran, and my encounter with the robber at Darak Beach was admittedly quite chilling for a naïve young traveler like myself. Undoubtedly, the police would be more experienced in detecting potential troublemakers, and if they happen to look like me that night, then they have the justification to pull me out of the bus. On the other hand, I also knew that no police officer was immune to bias, and perhaps their actions that night were motivated merely by the same negative stereotypes that others had told me about. What if by adapting so much to the ways of the people of Balochistan, I began to experience a teeny tiny slice of the hardships they endured on a constant basis? Verily, I am but a humble human unable to read minds, hence I admit that the intentions of the police officers that night is one of the many things I will never know for sure.

Fast forward. I was at the taxi stand in Qom, and my host desperately tried to negotiate with the driver of a shared taxi to take me directly to the airport without filling up the car with other passengers first. I had gone to the Holy Shrine for *maghrib* prayers together with my host's wife, and we nearly forgot I had to catch a flight that same evening. Admittedly, my host was not amused by the fact that our negligence had put him in the uncomfortable spot of arguing with a grumpy driver. After way too many rounds back and forth, I eventually agreed to pay triple the regular price, scraping together my last remaining tumans, while the driver agreed to take the loss of the fourth passenger who could have traveled in his car. With all disputes cleared, I loaded my bags—by now filled to the brim with Persian sweets—into the trunk and got into the car. The driver then removed the handbrake, pressed the gas pedal, and hit the road at maximum speed.

Just short of an hour later, I arrived at the crowded departure hall of Imam Khomeini Airport, just in time to check in to my flight. I had been invited to a wedding in Lahore, typically *desi* style at very short notice, and was now scrambling to make it back to Pakistan in time. This left me with little choice but to sacrifice the remaining few days of my dream journey and fly out of Tehran airport earlier than planned. There were still many places left in this country that I longed to see, and it hurt to cut the journey of a lifetime short, but at the same time I was also relieved that after weeks of arduous travel I could finally sit back and relax. My overland journey from Karachi to Tehran, while exciting, fun, insightful, and educational, had without a doubt drained every bit of energy out of me. It should come as no surprise that weeks of back to back overnight journeys in cramped buses running on a tight schedule left a mark on my physical health, but what was even more exhausting was the mental stress that came with adjusting to so many new people and places.

In three short weeks of travel, I had experienced more culture shocks than in my entire lifetime, and every single one seemed to be more intense than the one before. The sheltered lives of women in Balochistan, the adventurous experiences of their male counterparts, the clashing worldviews of urban Persians and the contrasts in standards of living, the discrimination and inequalities of all kinds that I witnessed had all left a profound impact on me. Not to mention the challenges of traveling alone across one of the world's most patriarchal places as a woman and the draining feeling that whatever I did was always wrong or insufficient. I was tired in every sense of the word and truly in need of a break in familiar territory.

Upon checking in, the airline staff scolded me for arriving so late. I had to skip lines in security and run to my gate, all the while being careful not to trip over my *chador*. The fact that I managed to board my flight on time was nothing short of a miracle; perhaps this was the reward for offering prayer at the Holy Shrine. I made it to my assigned seat before most other passengers had settled on board and made myself comfortable, even though I knew this first leg of my journey, to Dubai, would only be a short flight. Behind me, a group of young women around my age boarded the aircraft. Most of them were wearing long dresses and scarves so far at the back of their heads that most of their hair was exposed. About half of them had white bandages on their noses, revealing they had undergone a nose job during their visit to Iran. They were speaking Farsi to each other, but I could see blue passports reading "United States of America" in their designer purses.

Everyone took their seat and I half-heartedly listened to the standard flight-safety demonstration that I had nearly memorized by this point. Just ordinary things. What happened next, however, left me in surprise once again. As soon as the engines sounded, the women who had entered after me almost simultaneously ripped off their scarves and tore off their long dresses, leaving them in crop tops, hot pants, and heels. Dozens of passengers saw it, but no one batted an eye. Everyone continued to chat with their partners, scroll through their phones, flip through their magazines, and even the men across from the group of women focused their attention on the landscape outside of the windows rather than the generously exposed skin a few meters away—a world's difference from the staring man on the bus to Kerman. People seemed to mind their own business, and nobody worried about the "honor" of a group of girls, or the "bad influences" their behavior might spread to their daughters. Judging by the general atmosphere inside the cabin, it became abundantly clear that the mindsets of my fellow passengers differed radically from the people I had met in Balochistan, and all the behavior I had learned during my two-week-long transit no longer seemed appropriate. I looked around once more at the other women in the cabin and, soon enough, realized that in my full *hijab* and black *chador* I truly was the odd one out.

Tired from yet another overnight journey, I stumbled out of the aircraft, made my way through the neat hallways of Dubai International Airport, and proceeded to the immigration line before the clock struck four in the morning. I had a layover of about five hours and decided to leave the airport during this short time. When I exited the building, I was welcomed by a breeze of hot, humid air under a navy-blue sky. I knew that soon enough the sun would rise over the world's tallest building and transform the city into a literal oven that would roast me alive in my heat-absorbing black garments. Hence, I decided to call a taxi to take me to a nearby beach from where I could admire the sunrise.

By the time I stepped onto the sand at Al Mamzar Beach, I was sweating profusely, despite it being the coolest hour of the day. I gently lifted up my long black fabric and sat down to watch the sky transform into brighter shades by the minute. In front of me I saw calm water, gradually revealing its pristine clarity as the slowly rising sun illuminated the realm, and a captivating skyline in the background, whose lights appeared fainter and fainter in contrast. The sickle-shaped moon could barely hold onto its dominance of the Arabian sky, which became more crowded with cawing seagulls and the distant noises of airplane engines. Still, there were no people around, and I was all alone—until I spotted slight movements in the wet sand. I moved closer to the edge of the water and what I saw next blew my mind. A congregation of little golden starfish was moving under the shallow surface of the crystalline water until they eventually covered the entire stretch of beach!

Curious and utterly amazed to witness such a rare sight in the middle of one of the most modern metropolises in the world, I set aside my shoes and cautiously entered the water, trying not to get my *chador* wet. The sea was tropically warm but pleasantly refreshing against the hot air. I carefully took a step forward against the barely noticeable currents, and then another. Slowly, people began to flood into the sea, seemingly to engage in their morning exercise routines, and soon enough I heard bits of conversations in Tagalog far into the water coming from a group of elderly Filipino men practicing their swimming strokes. *How I wish I could swim just like them*, I pondered as I admired the laughing old men in wetsuits. Unfortunately, I could not. I was wearing long, dark clothes that would get all sandy and wet if I went any farther. I silently watched the men in the distance, who were soon joined by more swimmers.

As the sun slowly rose over the skyline and the city began to awaken, the urge to join the swimmers in the sea only grew stronger. Why am I even wearing my chador? I began to wonder as more and more men and women passed beside me. I was no longer in Balochistan, where my honor would be harmed and character would be judged by not wearing a large black cloth. I was in Dubai! I looked over my shoulder and saw that nobody was looking in my direction. Then, I carefully lifted my chadar and placed it in the sand, leaving me in a comfortable set of women's shalwar kameez, which was still very modest by most standards.

I took a couple of wide steps forward and plunged my chest into the clear turquoise sea, submerging myself in the refreshing warmth. Soon enough, my breaststrokes were in sync with the light waves, gently carrying me past the layers of golden sea stars until I eventually caught up with the crowd of swimmers at the horizon. Once again, I looked around, and found not a single pair of eyes staring at me. I was just one of the many swimmers on an early Dubai morning and what I was doing was nothing worthy of shame. In that moment I realized that although my time in Balochistan taught me many valuable lessons, I did not need to hold onto all of them, and now was a good time to let go of some.

AFTERWORD

Growing up as a non-minority in Germany, I learned to always speak my mind and recount my experiences without censoring them. During the process of writing this book, I came to realize that this is a great privilege that many do not possess. I learned that the stories I can tell without a second thought can have real-life consequences for the people on the ground. What may be a harmless anecdote to me as a traveler could cause significant problems for the ones who broke norms in the name of hospitality. They must deal with the social stigma and potentially even legal repercussions long after I leave, particularly in strict honor-based societies where a single act can tarnish a family's reputation for generations. Although I had been careful enough to conceal people's names and personal information from the beginning, I realized that sometimes, details may still be recognizable to local audiences. Hence, I spent over a year identifying, deleting, and rewriting parts of the book that may be considered sensitive in a local context.

Another obstacle I had to tackle throughout this book was navigating the inevitable political discourse when writing about a region as politically charged as Balochistan. Due to Balochistan's unstable situation and geopolitically significant location, many stakeholders constantly watch for any content that may fit their agenda. As a traveler whose only goal is to share my unique encounters from a female perspective, I have long stumbled around these roadblocks. It has been a dilemma trying to write what is on my mind while being aware of the adversity I may face from various sides for doing so. I want to reiterate that I in no way mean to criticize any particular stakeholders. Instead, I want to highlight some of the struggles faced by an undeniably strong people, praise their perseverance, and raise awareness of the vastly different realities lived by people around us.

Doing so, I recall the immense shock I felt when I found functioning air-conditioning in Dawood's village, realizing how accustomed I had become to the unavailability of basic resources and infrastructure in rural Pakistan. While for a short-term visitor like myself, the lack of electricity, running water, air-conditioning, quality medical care, and mobile signal present an annoyance at worst, these issues can be a matter of death for those who must spend their entire lives in these conditions. Besides the man who died from a simple injury due to the poor quality of medical facilities, which could treat only "fever" within a range of ten hours travel distance, whom I mentioned earlier in this book, I have met people who lost their children in the most unfortunate ways. There was a small settlement of serfs working on private land in the middle of the desert, where two children lost their lives due to heatstroke just the day before I visited. The family lived in a small collection of sheds unshielded from the 50 ℃ daytime heat, without electricity or running water. The settlement was located about two hours off-road by car from the nearest town with simple medical facilities, but the serfs had no vehicles to get around, only camels, and were left at the mercy of the local *sardars*. Another image I vividly recall is the beautiful smile of a Baloch woman I met in Karachi, who warmly welcomed me to her home and offered tea. I later learned that she had recently lost her young daughter in a blast during what she claimed were armed clashes between the military and rebels in her hometown. Other people I met seemed to constantly lose family members due to crime or feuds, receive threats from the perpetrators for speaking up, and some would even disappear into nothingness, never to be heard from again. Those who mourn the loss of family members due to violent crime spend many years in vain fighting for justice, as local legal systems can hardly be considered functional. My close friend, whose cousin was shot to death in an attempted robbery in 2022, is still waiting for developments in his case (as am I, victim of a horrific rape in 2022).

Balochistan is also heavily affected by natural calamities such as droughts and floods. The most notable example of this may be the "super floods" of 2022, which devastated large areas of southern Pakistan and killed thousands of people from landslides, drowning, starvation, and waterborne diseases, and displaced millions. As the living conditions were already deplorable during my visit shortly prior, the severity of the humanitarian crisis left behind by this disaster is beyond my imagination. Rumors about international donations not reaching their destinations due to corruption and looting are heart-breaking, but what infuriates me the most is that the exorbitant carbon emissions released by corporations from the Global North are the likely cause for this catastrophe, as there is a highly probable link between the global climate crisis and increasingly extreme weather events that disproportionately impact underprivileged populations in the Global South.

Lastly, some people, especially women, in the region are subject to extreme cultural restrictions. While I am in no position to criticize traditional practices or norms, murdering in the name of "honor" is an undeniably condemnable yet shockingly prevalent act. Primarily women, but sometimes men, may face the bullet for reasons like talking to the opposite gender, wearing clothing of their choice, dancing, pursuing a career, marrying the person of their choice, refusing marriage proposals, serving cold food, and other acts that their families believe to be wrong. Notions of "proper" and "improper" conduct may appear shocking to some, as can be seen in the case of Jalal's family in Chapter 2, where the girls were expected to stay inside the house all day, as going outside was considered bad even if fully covered, or Mureed's family in Chapter 4, where only men had access to the internet under the notion that women should not be able to communicate with people outside of their family. Although many attempt to justify such practices in the name of religion, this explanation is as erroneous as it could get, as Islam unquestionably advocates for the equality of all people and strictly outlaws violence against women.

Given the myriad challenges faced by people in Balochistan, one may wonder: *why not just leave?* Why do people not leave behind such hardship and migrate to a better place? As you may already be expecting at this point, things are not as easy for most. Apart from the immense pain many would feel leaving behind their beloved motherland that their ancestors had inhabited for generations, simply moving to another place is practically impossible for most. Ravaged by poverty and often left without access to primary education, self-sufficiency is the key to survival for many. Without the stable income and housing of their homeland, many migrants are forced to settle in illegal urban slums known as *katchi abadis*, where living conditions may be even worse than back home. As for the more fortunate ones who can afford to move to the big cities under stable conditions, discrimination based on various factors still prevails, impacting their chances of finding suitable jobs, housing, and dignified social life. Being able to "simply leave" is yet another privilege that many of us possessing it take for granted.

Yet despite these countless obstacles, I never fail to be impressed by the Baloch people's immense strength, courage, and perseverance. The most creative, intelligent, and impactful artists and thinkers I know are Baloch, hailing from the streets of Lyari to the villages of Makran. Even under the most modest circumstances, they find a way to excel at what they do, but if they are provided with the right opportunities, their skills blossom to another level. I hope that in the future, these talented and inspiring people will be provided with more opportunities, from access to education and basic resources in the countryside to cultural spaces, scholarships, and investment in art and innovation in the cities. I have seen extraordinary potential in the people I have met and am convinced that they will provide great enrichment to society if provided the platforms to do so.

I am beyond grateful for the incredible privilege that allows me to travel the world and witness these stories. Traveling has undoubtedly been my greatest source of knowledge, wisdom, and inspiration, and I would not want to trade this fortune for anything else in the world. However, I am also painstakingly aware of how inaccessible travel is for the vast majority of people in the world, which was my greatest motivation for writing this book. I want my experiences to enrich not only myself but also the minds of others. I hope that by sharing these stories, readers can become aware of the many differences and inequalities that people face around the world, and I aim to inspire people to make small changes in their thinking and actions so that, slowly but surely, we can see this world move towards a better direction.

Once again, huge thanks for reading *Of Threads and Needles*, and I hope to see you in my next book!

ABOUT BALOCHI EMBROIDERY

A contribution by Gohar Malik

Embroidered pillowcase in a Balochi home.

Balochi embroidery is an ancient art form unique to the region of Balochistan, characterized by heavily embroidered textiles featuring a myriad of geometric shapes. It is believed to originate from the Mehrgarh civilization, an ancient farming society founded around 7000 BC in northeastern Balochistan. Since then, the craft has been passed down from generation to generation and continues to be practiced extensively by Baloch women until this day. Many women pick up thread and needle at tender ages and spend every free minute practicing the art up until the old age. This makes them not only some of the world's most skilled craftswomen but also custodians of Balochi culture and identity.

Balochi embroidery is dominated by two main styles known as *Dooch* and *Bedooch*. *Dooch* consists of a traditional assortment of seven vibrant colors known as *haft ranga*: white, black, red, orange, green, and blue, as well as the color of the textile. *Bedooch* on the other hand is characterized by a different assortment of colors and designs, including non-traditional colors such as pink and purple. Furthermore, styles vary from region to region. For example, the region of Noshki is particularly known for mirrorwork incorporated in embroidery, whereas Makran is known for the *Mosoom* design, which incorporates nature patterns that reflect the seasons of the year.

ABOUT BALOCHI DRESSES

An unstitched Balochi women's suit consisting of *pashk*, *shalwar*, and *chadar*

Traditional Balochi women's suits consist of baggy trousers (*shalwar*), a dress (*pashk*), and a headscarf (*dupatta* or *chadar*). The *pashk* contains characteristic embroidered portions, including a chest piece (*jeegh*), a pocket (*pendol*), as well as additional lines of embroidery on the sides (*patt*) and bottom (*daman*). Balochi suits come in a vast variety of styles and materials, ranging from everyday clothes to expensive wedding dresses.

Observing the intricate patterns, one cannot ignore the endless amount of hard work that goes into each dress. From selecting the fabrics and designing to patterns to the meticulous needlework of filling every inch of fabric with colorful threads, handmade Balochi dresses typically takes months to complete and can sell for the equivalent of hundreds of US dollars on the markets. However, most dresses are made by families for personal use and enrich the colorful closets of Baloch families.

Jewelry made from old embroidery pieces being sold to tourists at Chabahar's Salt Lake

Thanks to the heavy embroidery protecting the fabric, Balochi dresses tend to be very durable and can survive many decades being exposed to harsh conditions. This allows treasured family heirlooms to be passed on from generation to generation. The combination of labor-intensive production and long shelf life presents the direct opposite to modern-day fast fashion.

Even when the fabric of the dress eventually gives in to the forces of the elements, the embroidered portions tend to stay intact for significantly longer, allowing them to be reused in a variety of ways such as jewelry and decoration pieces. This reduces wastes even further, making Balochi dresses the epitome of sustainable fashion.

And when a family does decide to clean out their closet, old dresses almost always end up in the hands of someone else. Thanks to the great generosity of Baloch people, many choose to donate their clothes to the needy, who in turn benefit from the high-quality material for a long time. Unfortunately, this charitable dynamic has resulted in prejudiced perceptions by outsiders. In cities like Karachi, many women beggars can be seen wearing Balochi dresses, which in turn prompts people to associate Balochi embroidery with poverty and look down on this precious millennia-old craft.

CULTURAL APPRECIATION OR APPROPRIATION?

Balochi pashk used as a decoration piece in a tourist hotel in Cappadocia, Turkey.

Unfortunately, the deep history and culture behind Balochi clothing is not widely recognized as the ethnic group continues to face discrimination. This attitude is especially prevalent in the fashion scene, where non-Baloch individuals and entities can be seen profiting off Balochi traditions without any form of acknowledgement or compensation. The perhaps most common offenders are Pakistani fashion brands, which oftentimes mimic the shapes and patterns of Balochi embroidery without appropriate credits. For example, one brand carelessly imitated Balochi *dooch* through print designs and marketed the work as 'Kashmiri embroidery', implying the patterns are native to the Himalayan region of Kashmir.

The issue of cultural appropriation extends beyond fashion brands to individual use as well. I personally have seen photos of white Western women on social media wearing Balochi *pashk* without *shalwar* like a summer dress, accompanied by misleading captions such as 'vintage Afghani gypsy dress' or 'boho fashion'. Souvenir vendors in tourist hotspots within and even outside of Pakistan tend to sell vintage Balochi dresses at inflated costs without a single mention of Balochistan, implying the art is native to the place of sale, oftentimes thousands of kilometers away from its motherland.

These instances of cultural appropriation are extremely harmful as the cherry-picking and misrepresentation of Baloch identity further pushes back the recognition of an already oppressed group and adds fuel to widespread social inequalities. But does that mean outsiders should stay away from Balochi embroidery completely or is there a way to appreciate the art without being exploitative?

The answer is yes to the latter. Most Baloch people, including myself, appreciate non-Baloch people wearing our traditional dress as long as they acknowledge the origins of our rich traditions. We hold no grudge against anyone who owns our dresses and we love seeing our culture being presented to the world in a positive light. However, we do ask you to wear our outfits in their intended way (please don't go shalwar-less!) and give credit to Baloch culture for these beautiful designs. This marks the fine but important line between *cultural appreciation* and *cultural appropriation.*

ACKNOWLEDGMENTS

First and foremost, my greatest thanks goes to everyone who has helped me realize my lifelong dream of traveling across Balochistan and Iran by road. In particular, I would like to thank Jalal and his family; Usman, Imran, and Dur Bibi; Mureed and his family; Moslem and his family; Mohamed (yes, even him); J&J; Mehdi; and the rest of the Iranian Couchsurfing community, and everyone who is not mentioned in this book. Without a doubt, this journey would have been all but impossible without your guidance and hospitality, and I would not be the same person if it were not for you. I don't know if you will ever read this, but your smiles have a special place in my heart and I pray that they will continue to brighten your faces every day of your lives.

I also want to express my gratitude to my wonderful Baloch friends who were not directly part of this journey but helped me immensely in getting to know this rich culture and traditions. Special thanks go to my dear girlfriends, who granted me the deepest insights into Baloch women's culture; the talented artists who alongside promoting their culture and language were also immense motivation for nurturing my creative soul; and the deeply knowledgeable Gohar Malik, who contributed a section about Balochi dresses and embroidery to this book. Your wisdom is unmatched by any lexicon or database, and I'm humbled that you have taken the time to answer my questions to make this book as accurate and informative as possible.

I feel beyond grateful for my wonderful family, particularly my parents, who have always supported my dreams to see the world and pursue my creative passion. Thank you for raising me to become such a strong, independent, and sometimes a-little-too-stubborn young woman. Ever since I was born, you have encouraged me to venture out and admire the world around me, study books, arts, and the sciences. You never made me feel like I had to act a certain way simply because I was a girl, and you taught me not to worry too much about society's norms. Thank you for instilling awareness about the cultural sensitivities that are ever so important in this increasingly globalized world. Our trips to churches and mosques, temples and synagogues, and our shared meals full of spices from around the world are the very experiences that made me the open-minded and tolerant person I am today. Thank you for allowing me to see the world from this lens!

Lastly, I want to acknowledge all the professionals who have helped me bring this book into existence. All too often we tend to overlook the many steps that transform a lackluster first draft into the treasured gems adorning our bookshelves. Thank you to all my editors, proofreaders, and designers who worked in the background to make *Of Threads and Needles* possible!

And of course, huge thanks to everyone who has read this far! I feel honored by your interest in my story and I sincerely hope to see you again in my next book!

GLOSSARY

abaya – a long robe that can be worn on top of other clothes

Alhamdulillah – "Praise be to God," a phrase commonly used by Muslims to express gratitude

Allah hafiz – "May God protect," good bye

Assalamoaleikum – "Peace be upon you," a common greeting among Muslims

Astaghfirullah – "I seek forgiveness from God," an expression of shame or disapproval

Baloch – an ethnic group inhabiting parts of modern-day Pakistan, Iran, and Afghanistan; a person of said ethnicity

Balochi – adj. of "Baloch"; language of the Baloch people

Balochistan – a region divided across modern-day Pakistan, Iran, and Afghanistan primarily inhabited by the Baloch people; southwestern province of Pakistan

banuk – Balochi for "lady"; a respectful way to address a woman

biryani – a spiced rice dish containing meat or vegetables

chadar/chador – a large cloak covering head and body, spelled differently in Pakistani/Balochi and Persian context

chai – milk-based spiced black tea (Pakistan); plain black tea (Iran)

charpai – a traditional four-footed woven bed common across South Asia

chillim – a type of wooden hookah commonly used in Balochistan

Couchsurfing – an online platform designed to connect travelers with locals for the purpose of cultural exchange. Locals typically offer to host travelers in their homes free of cost as a gesture of hospitality.

CPEC – China-Pakistan Economic Corridor: a bilateral project between the governments of Pakistan and China aiming to improve Pakistan's infrastructure and facilitate trade for China. The initiative includes large-scale projects like the construction of Gwadar Port.

Desi – relating to South Asian culture

dooch – traditional Balochi embroidery

doochi – containing *dooch*

dupatta – a scarf smaller than a *chadar*, often used as a headscarf

fajr – the earliest of the five daily prayers obligatory for Muslims, performed at sunrise

gutka – a type of chewing tobacco made from betel nut, tobacco, and other ingredients popular across South Asia

halal – permissible for Muslims

hammam – a historical public bathhouse common in the Middle East

haram – impermissible for Muslims

hijab – the Islamic principle of modesty in terms of dress and behavior, applicable to both women and men; modest dress; commonly used to refer to the head covering of Muslim women

insha'Allah – "God willing," oftentimes synonymous with "hopefully"

Iranic – a language family and its speakers, including the Baloch, Persians, Pashtuns, Kurds, and more

Islamic Republic of Iran – the state of Iran under the theocratic government that succeeded the Iranian Revolution in 1979

jinn – invisible creatures in Islamic mythology, oftentimes equated to ghosts

Karachiite – a person from Karachi

katchi abadi – an urban slum

kheer – a sweet milk rice dessert common across South Asia

Kurd – an Iranic ethnic group inhabiting primarily parts of Türkiye, Syria, Iraq, Iran, and Armenia

Kurdistan – the land primarily inhabited by the Kurds

Lasi – a dialect of Sindhi with significant influence of the Balochi language spoken by the people of Lasbela, considered a separate language by some

maghrib – the fourth of the five daily prayers obligatory for Muslims, performed at sunset

Makran – a region marking southern, coastal portion of Balochistan

Makrani – pertaining to Makran; a dialect of Balochi spoken by the locals of said area

masha'Allah – "What God has willed," expression of a positive reaction

mehndi – a temporary tattoo typically applied on hand and feet with henna paste; a function of a South Asian wedding during which henna is traditionally applied

naan – a type of bread commonly accompanying meals across South Asia; Balochi for "food"

namkeen rosh – a dish consisting of soft-boiled meat

nikkah – Islamic marriage contract; the function of a wedding when such contract is signed

niqab – a face shield covering everything but the eyes worn by some Muslim women for modesty

pardah – the custom of gender segregation practiced in parts of South Asia through the segregation of public spaces, uses of curtains, fully covering clothing, and traditional gender roles that tend to assign women tasks performed inside the house

pashk – a heavily embroidered upper body garment part of the traditional Balochi women's suit

Pashtun – an Iranic ethnic group inhabiting primarily the northwest of Pakistan and Afghanistan

pendol – the characteristic embroidered front pocket on Balochi *pashk*

Persia – used in this book to describe the primarily Persian-inhabited parts of Iran

Persian – the predominant ethnic group in Iran, primarily Farsi-speaking

rilli – a traditional type of blanket characterized by patch-work designs found across southern Pakistan

Rind – a major caste among the Baloch people

rupee – referring to the Pakistani Rupee, the currency of Pakistan

sajji – a Balochi dish consisting of meat cooked over an open flame

sardar – a feudal landlord and tribal chief in Balochistan; a title denoting nobility

sawas – traditional Balochi woven sandals with smooth, flat soles

shalwar – baggy trousers accompanying both men's and women's outfits across South Asia. Baloch men are particularly known for wearing very baggy *shalwar*

shalwar kameez – an outfit consisting of *shalwar* and a long top (*kameez*). Typically worn by both men and women in most of Pakistan, while Baloch women tend to wear *doochi* suits

Sindhi – an ethnic group primarily inhabiting the southeastern regions of Pakistan along the Indus River; the language spoken by said ethnic group

Sistan and Baluchestan – southeastern province of Iran encompassing the country's share of Balochistan

Shia – one of the two major branches of Islam, practiced primarily in Iran, Iraq, and other parts of the world

sohan halwa – a South Asian sweet dish with a buttery base

Sunni – one of the two major branches of Islam, widely practiced around the world including most of Pakistan and Balochistan

taarof – the Persian custom of refusing a gift multiple times before accepting it

takya – cylinder-shaped, oftentimes embroidered pillows commonly found in Balochistan

tharki – used across South Asia to describe a creep, someone desperate for attention from the opposite gender

tuman – 10 Iranian Rial, the most popular way to count the currency of Iran *waleeg* – a collection of gold rings worn out the outer cartilage of the ear by married Baloch women

Zoroastrian – the predominant religion in Persia before the introduction of Islam. It is practiced to this day by a minority in Iran and respected by many Persians.

ABOUT THE AUTHOR

Arabela (Bela) Urpi Iggesen Valenzuela is a German-Peruvian-American author, businesswoman, and travel blogger behind The Spicy Travel Girl. *Of Threads and Needles* is the first out of a series of travel memoirs from her time living and traveling through Pakistan as a young adult.

Currently pursuing a Bachelor's degree in Molecular Bioscience at Duke Kunshan University, Arabela's interests extend far beyond science. She believes herself to have gathered most of her knowledge during her travels to more than sixty countries around the globe. As an intrepid solo female traveler, Arabela's mission is to empower women through travel and promote lesser known parts of the world. Her work also draws attention to the inequalities she witnesses on her journeys as well as the cultural richness of the places she visits. After having lived in Germany, the United States, and Pakistan, Arabela now calls China her home. When she is not on the road or in a classroom, Arabela is likely busy feeding stray cats, studying new languages, or recreating one of the countless delicious dishes she has tried during her travels.

Follow Arabela's adventures on social media
@thespicytravelgirl and her website
www.thespicytravelgirl.com !

Claim a FREE copy of Bela's Top 10 Travel Insider Tips!

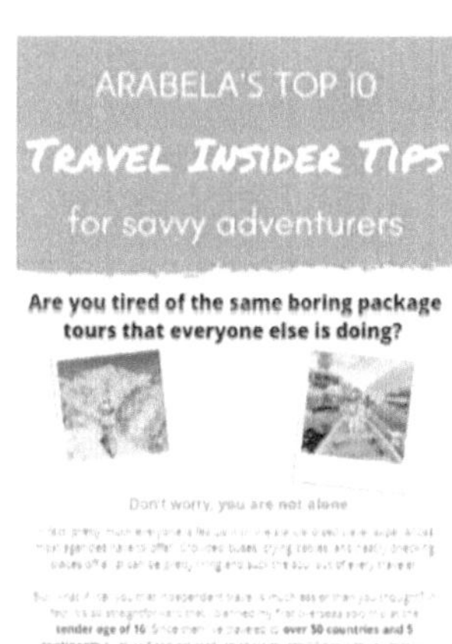
ARABELA'S TOP 10
TRAVEL INSIDER TIPS
for savvy adventurers
Are you tired of the same boring package tours that everyone else is doing?
Don't worry, you are not alone

www.thespicytravelgirl.com

www.ingramcontent.com/pod-product-compliance
Lightning Source LLC
Chambersburg PA
CBHW020241130626
46549CB00005B/1997